THE CHANGING FACE OF THE ASIAN CONSUMER
Insights and Strategies for Asian Markets

Bernd Schmitt

THE CHANGING FACE OF THE ASIAN CONSUMER
Insights and Strategies for Asian Markets

10 9 8 7 6 5 4 3 2 1
CTP MPM
20 16 15 14 13

When ordering this title, use
ISBN 978-1-259-07101-0 or MHID 1-259-07101-4.

Printed in Singapore

CONTENTS

Asia is one of the fastest growing regions today and its future outlook is strong. To be sure, there may be setbacks, but the long-term trend seems positive.

Asian consumer markets are increasingly fueling this growth. As a result, Asian consumers have become prime targets of multinational corporations and Asian firms alike.

As a manager, you are well aware that competition in this dynamic part of the world is fierce and that you need detailed consumer insight to succeed. This book will provide you with an understanding of the changing face of the Asian consumer. I will show you how insights into Asian consumer behavior can result in profitable strategies for Asian markets.

I have been active in East Asia—the region ranging from China to Indonesia, and from India to South Korea, Japan, and the Philippines, which I will be covering in this book—as a researcher, speaker, and consultant for more than 20 years. This book is therefore not only based on second-hand research but also on my own research, field work and experiences with Asian consumers and companies. Over the years, I have been a visiting professor and given speeches and seminars in mainland China, India, Indonesia, Hong Kong, Japan, Malaysia, South Korea, Singapore, Taiwan, and the Philippines. I have also written cases and done consulting projects for Chinese, Japanese, Korean, and Southeast Asian companies.

From July 2011 until June 2013, while I wrote this book, I lived for two years in Singapore, as the inaugural executive director of the new Institute on Asian Consumer Insight (ACI). The Institute helps companies develop growth strategies based on insights about Asian consumers and Asian markets. ACI was set up by the Singapore Economic Development Board (EDB) and is located within the Nanyang Business School of Nanyang Technological University. I would like to thank Thien Kwee Eng and her team at EDB as well as my own staff at ACI for their support. Shireen Seow read and edited all the chapters. Kishan Golyan did background research and designed the figures for the strategy tools. Rachel Samuil and Jarene Ang provided research support. Some of the cases and business examples have been featured earlier at ACI's Asia Business Summit and in ACI's Asia Business Insights journal. Here and there in the book, I am also referring to research insights created by the researchers associated with the institute.

In addition, I thank the editorial team at McGraw-Hill for their encouragement and support for this project. A special thank to Jacinta Ong for editing the book flap. I would also like to thank Ark Studio who created the graphic layout and cartoons for the book. Finally, as in all of my recent book projects, my Asian-European-American boy Thomas, who is about to become a teenager, helped me greatly. Thomas, my staff and I took all the photos in this book. He also gave me feedback and helped me finish the manuscript.

Singapore, September 2013
Bernd Schmitt

View from my Singapore apartment (from right to left): the old (container port), the new (financial district), the very new (entertainment).

section 1:
ASIAN IN

In the first section of this book, I will provide insights and findings on Asia's growing markets, its rising middle class, the collectivist mind and shopper behavior. In addition, I will present various techniques for gaining consumer insights.

Let's light up the bulbs!

SIGHTS

We will begin with a "macro" insight that drives business in Asia today: The Asian consumer has arrived and will be gaining further prominence throughout this century. In fact, in the future the Asian consumer will be at par, or may even replace, the Western consumer as the focal point of all marketing and business.

Next, I will provide insight into Asia's rising middle class, and try to define and understand it. Afterwards we will examine the Asian collectivist mind and determine why Asians are becoming more and more individualistic. In addition, we will examine the Asian shopper, and what makes them tick. We will learn that Asian consumers are driven by three seemingly incompatible desires that clever managers and marketers need to understand to be successful in the Asian region.

I will conclude by discussing techniques and methodologies for gaining consumer insight, and offer my views on these methodologies. Because Asian consumers are changing so fast, all research and intelligence about Asian consumers are only snapshots that need to be fine-tuned and revised as new data and information become available.

Taken together, the insights and methodologies discussed in the first section of this book provide a valuable framework and roadmap for identifying the key opportunities in Asian markets.

01

THE MACRO PICTURE
THE CENTURY OF THE ASIAN CONSUMER

As the spotlight will be increasingly on Asia, businesses need to understand the changing face of the Asian consumer

When I first arrived in Asia in 1991 to teach a course on consumer behavior in a run-down shack in the western district of Beijing, China, I would not have thought that the 21st century would be called the "Asian century." The bubble of the Japanese economy had burst. Korean products were perceived as cheap and low quality. Nobody was talking about India and Indonesia as economic forces.

Soon thereafter, things began to change. The Asian tiger economies (Hong Kong, Singapore, South Korea, and Taiwan) grew at a rapid pace, spurred largely by industrial policies to export to rich, industrialized nations such as the United States and European countries. Thailand, Indonesia, and the Philippines were not far behind, and China took a great leap forward.

Then, however, came the first setback: the 1997 Asian Financial Crisis. It began in Thailand with currency devaluation, and spread from South Asia to North Asia. South Korea, a star performer during the previous years, required the intervention of the International Monetary Fund (IMF). Economic growth slowed in the other Asian markets. But the crisis also resulted in reforms. Just a few years later, around the turn of the new millennium, triggered by the technology revolution of the internet, growth picked up again. This time it was interrupted by the bust of the dot-com bubble and then by the 2008 Global Financial Crisis.

The Asian century

Since 2010 talk of the Asian century has resumed. This time, most economists argue that things are drastically different from the 1990s and 2000s. Numerous economic studies have identified East Asia—the region ranging from China to Indonesia and from India to Korea and the Philippines—as the major growth engine for the world economy for decades to come.

We will see. Based on my two decades of experience in Asia I am a bit more skeptical. The overall trend in this century will be positive but there may be bumps on the way. For example, at the time of this writing, Asian emerging markets, and, in particular, India and Indonesia, are under severe pressure.

Nonetheless, a 2011 study by the Asian Development Bank found that within the next few decades an additional 3 billion Asians could enjoy living standards similar to those in Europe and the United States today. The Asian region could account for over half of global output by the middle of this century. Growth figures for East Asia (excluding Japan) typically range from 5 to 6.5 per cent, and even higher for certain individual markets. Even if these growth figures turned out to be slightly lower, Asia must be a key priority for many companies, from multinational corporations to medium-sized and smaller businesses based in Asia.

The term "Asian century" has been used to describe the projected 21st-century dominance of Asian politics, economy, and culture that parallels the characterization of the 20th century as the "American century." *Megatrends: The World in 2050*, published by *The Economist*, arrives at the following bold prediction: by 2050, Asia will have re-emerged as the dominant force of the world economy. At the focus are two economies in particular: China and India.

> *From a historical perspective, China's emerging status as the world's leading economy will not be a novelty. It was by far the world's largest economy until the 19th century (in terms of purchasing power parity) accounting for 20–30 per cent of the world's output. Along with India, it dominated the world economy for nearly two millennia … By 2050, these two economies will have resumed that dominance. If the forecast presented here is anywhere near right, developing Asia as a whole will by mid-century account for something close to half of the world's output. Prepare for the Asian century.*
> *(Megatrends, p. 180)*

In 2001, the investment bank Goldman Sachs coined the term BRIC (Brazil, Russia, India, China), arguing that by 2050, their combined economies would overtake those of the world's richest countries. Many would argue that Goldman Sachs could have just as well written about China alone.

Indeed, China has been the star performer over the last three decades. The world's fastest growing major economy, and arguably its most dynamic, China has grown on average approximately 9 per cent annually since 1979 when it embarked on its open door policy and began experimenting with capitalism and market forces. It has lifted over 620 million of its people out of extreme poverty— more than 100 per cent of what the world as a whole has done in total. In 2010, China became the world's second-largest economy, overtaking Germany, the United Kingdom, France, and all the rest of Western Europe.

The economic performance of India, the other billion-people nation on the planet has been far shakier. In 1991, the state was almost bankrupt. From 2003 to 2008 it experienced a boom with growth rates of 8-9 per cent. In 2013, it experienced the next crisis. One might argue that Indonesia is similar to India in terms of its potentials and troubles. In sum, while Asia overall, and in particular China has a positive outlook in the long term, there are other nations that remain question marks.

Shifting the economic center of gravity

Danny Quay, Professor of Economics and International Development at the London School of Economics, has visually plotted the predicted shift of the global economy and the rise (or re-emergence) of the East. Specifically, Professor Quay depicts the global economy's center of gravity as the average location of economic activity across geographies on earth. To calculate the global economy's center of gravity, he uses income and geographical location data across nearly 700 identifiable places on the planet. In the 1980s, the economic center of gravity was mid-Atlantic between the United States and Western Europe. By 2010, because of the rise of China, India, and the rest of East Asia, the center of gravity had shifted to a location east of Helsinki and Bucharest. Extrapolating growth, Professor Quay found that the economic center of gravity will drift further East, and by 2050, will have moved from its 1980 location 9,300 km to the east or 1.5 times the radius of the planet to a point between China and India.

This shift is likely to have major policy implications. Policy formulation for the world economy and global governance will no longer be the domain of the last century's rich countries but will be more strongly shaped by the East. One of the questions, which have been fiercely debated among economists and policy makers, is whether this will be good for the West—and for the world.

In *The Aid Watch* – a now closed-down blog by New York University's Development Research Institute – William Easterly, a Professor of Economics at New York University, assumed the role of official spokesman for the West, arguing that "the richer are our trading partners, other things equal, the more demand for our products, the more and better jobs created thereby, the more gains from trade, the more innovation as the extent of the world market grows, and the more we can benefit from the additional human capital and innovation happening in the East … In sum, what's not to like?" Others on the blog have disagreed, arguing that the West and other parts of the world should not, through technology transfer and investments, subsidize the East's development. Easterly, too, cautioned, "If one day the East as a whole could have a greater influence on the global economy than the U.S., it could change everything we know about how politics, development, and the world as a whole work."

Dark clouds on the horizon
Another question that is debated is whether growth in Asia will in

Hazy skies, shady waters...

fact continue and result in world dominance by 2050 (if not earlier) or whether dark clouds are on the horizon. Are we witnessing a growth miracle in Asia based on solid policy, or was what has happened thus far simply luck?

In the early 1990s, William Easterly, together with economists Michael Kremer, Lant Pritchett, and Larry Summers wrote a much noted article on the drivers of long-term growth, titled "Good Policy or Good Luck?" They pointed out that strong growth performance in one decade was absolutely no guarantee of fast growth the next. In fact, there was almost no relationship between country growth rates over time. Past performance did not guarantee future success. Growth miracles, the authors concluded, were just good luck.

Yet, currently economists seem to favor the "good policy" point of view. Take China, in particular. Many economists predict that significant growth will continue until 2030. In 2010, the Asian Development Bank projected that China might grow at a 5.5 per cent average during the two decades to 2030. As former IMF economist Arvind Subramanian points out in his book *Eclipse*, a growth rate of 5.5 per cent would mean that China's per capita income (at purchasing power parity) would be around USD 33,000 by 2030—up from around USD 11,000 in 2010, and about the same as current per capita income in the European Union. As a whole, the Chinese economy would be about twice the size of the U.S. economy. Moreover, growth may very well be higher, especially if China continues to improve education, research and development, and property rights. So the Asian century looks likely to be a reality.

Is the consumption revolution coming?

To date, most of the Asian growth story has not been driven by consumer markets, however. Consider again China. As elsewhere in Asia, China's growth has been the result of exports and heavy investment in infrastructure and manufacturing. State-owned enterprises continue to be at the center of the domestic economy. Moreover, in recent years, China has accumulated a large trade surplus with the rest of the world, particularly the United States and Europe, and over USD 1 trillion in foreign currency reserves.

Yet, after 30 years of rapid growth, China is beginning to restructure. China understands that to maintain its pace of economic growth, it must shift from external demand to domestic demand, from government investment to private investment, and from investment-driven growth to consumer-led growth. While overall consumption figures are still low and the saving rate is high, per capita real consumption, adjusted for inflation, has increased by 80 per cent since 2005. Moreover, there are already some mind-boggling consumption figures: with a population of 1.3 billion people, China has 900 million mobile phone users; 370 million households have television, and the number of annual car sales is higher than in any other nation.

This emerging consumption phenomenon is likely to continue, as the middle class continues to grow. A 2010 study by the OECD Development Center, combining household survey data with growth projections for 145 countries, shows that Asia accounts for less than one-quarter of today's middle class. But they predict that by 2020, that share could double, with China and India driving the trend. More than half the world's middle class could then be in Asia, and Asian consumers could account for over 40 per cent of global middle class consumption. In fact, a large mass of Asian households have already incomes that position them just below the global middle class.

As millions of people are pulled out of poverty and enter the middle class, they will become first-time consumers. As their incomes and purchasing power increase further, they will replace first-tier basic products with branded goods and engage in lifestyle, and even luxury consumption. Along the way, Asian consumers will become picky and choosy, expecting top-notch products and services that make them happy. The rise of the Asian middle class, with its endless appetite for more and more and better and better consumer products and brands, spells huge opportunities for companies and their brands. Western companies and brands like Coca-Cola, Colgate, Nestlé, PepsiCo, Procter & Gamble, Unilever, and Volkswagen have already claimed their stake in Asian consumer markets—and many companies from Japan and other Asian markets have as well. They are all expanding in the region. Moreover, companies are designing increasingly sophisticated products for Asian consumers, and some believe that the "creative economy" will soon be a big thing all across Asia.

Economists also speculate that there will be increasing scope for mergers and acquisitions in the consumer goods industries, with multinational players buying out entrenched local brands to expand their product lines. On the local front, some Asian brands have also achieved the scale to acquire some global brands. For example, India's Tata Group has made major acquisitions in the auto sector (buying out Land Rover and Jaguar) as well as in beverages (purchasing Tetley Tea and Good Earth Herbal Tea in the United States, among others). Chinese consumer company giants have also shown signs of being active: for instance, Lenovo has bought out the laptop division of IBM, and Geely Motors has bought Volvo. As Indian and Chinese companies strengthen their global management capabilities, more acquisitions of consumer brands and products will follow in the years to come.

What's next?

What does all this mean for Asian consumers?

Asian consumers will feel that their time has arrived. Throughout the second half of the 20th century, American shoppers were ruling. They were the reference point, the focal point for all business and marketing. If you had made it then in the United States with American consumers, you had a good chance to be successful anywhere.

This may change in the 21st century. The Asian century may very well turn out to be the century of the Asian consumer. As a result, companies will need insights into the changing face of the Asian consumer in order to launch strategies to succeed in Asian markets.

02

CONSUMER PROFILE
ASIA'S FAST RISING MIDDLE CLASS

The middle class is the foundation of a modern economy and the key to sustainable economic development in Asia. But who is part of the middle class, and what do middle class consumers want and desire when their incomes rise?

Mention Asian business, economy, or consumers, and the issue of "Asia's fast rising middle class" will emerge. The middle class is the foundation of any modern economy and society. It is essential for sustainable economic development. Without it, a market-oriented economy cannot thrive. In sum, an economy can only be sustained in the long run if it has a mass group of middle-class consumers.

The life of a middle class consumer

Eight years ago, Pham Hia Vien moved from his village in the south to the prosperous city of Ho Chi Minh, where he now lives with his parents, wife and daughter in an 750-sq ft apartment in the older part of town.

Pham Hia Vien, 35, is a computer software provider in a company he opened with his friend a couple of years ago. He brings in an annual income of USD 21,000, placing his family right in the middle of the city's middle class. Pham Hia Vien spends half of his income on food and housing, though his family also spends a lot on transportation and entertainment. In the past few years, his wife has begun buying groceries at a new supermarket instead of from the local convenience store, and the family buys electronics from a local mall. They now have USD 4,000 in household assets, including a washing machine, a refrigerator, a television, a microwave oven, a DVD player and three mobile phones—all of which, with the exception of the refrigerator, are international brands. Pham Hia Vien owns a motorcycle, which he bought for USD 700.

The family has seen a dramatic upgrade in the quality of their lives in the last few years, and they have high hopes for their future. Pham Hia Vien expects his income to double within the next five years, and he and his wife are already planning how their lives will change. Their first focus is on housing. The family currently lives in an neighborhood with narrow streets and older, worn buildings, and they would prefer a more developed area. They have been looking at a house with greater investment value and more living and outdoor space, including a backyard and a parking spot. They have decided that they will fully air-condition and heat their new home, and are budgeting USD 10,000 for new furniture. They then plan to invest in a small car and, eventually, new office space for Pham Hia Vien's

Definitely a member of the middle class

company, ideally in one of the commercial developments that have recently sprouted up in the city. The family also expects to spend more on healthcare and, as their daughter grows up, education and leisure travel.

This story depicts the wants and aspiration of a family in Vietnam. Such stories are becoming a norm all over Asia, from India and China to Indonesia, Malaysia, Thailand and the Philippines.

Most companies understand the importance of the middle class. They know the middle class is the key to their future business growth in Asia. As a result, they are keen on identifying and targeting this segment. Yet, while there has been much excitement and hype, there is also much debate and confusion over who and what make up Asia's middle class.

What does it mean to be middle class?

Little consensus exists on the specific parameters that define the middle class. In the field of economics alone, multiple definitions of middle class are used. Moreover, there are other definitions based on occupation and lifestyle. And asking the people—that is, consumers—to define who is part of the Asian middle class and who is not doesn't help. A study with 500 respondents across Asian cities revealed that consumers were confused and could not clearly define "what the low, middle, or high income is. All the investigated cities lack a definition that a majority of people would agree with," the report concluded.

Some economists use an absolute measure for the middle class. That way, the middle class has been defined, in 2005 purchasing power parity terms in USD, as people earning between USD 2 and USD 20 per day (e.g., by academic researchers Banerjee and Duflo), between USD 2 and USD 20 per day (e.g., in a 2010 Asian Development Bank study), and between USD 10 and USD 100 per day (in a 2010 OECD study). Other economists have defined the middle class in relative terms, for example, in terms of percentiles of an income distribution (say, the 20th and 80th percentiles) or in terms of the shape of the distribution or distribution around a mean (say, 75–125 per cent of the median income distribution of a country). Finally, some economists have stated that in developing countries the middle class lies between the median poverty line of developing countries and the poverty line of the United States.

Different measures can produce vastly different results. So it is important to pay attention to the fine print next time you read an article on the rise of the middle class. Specifically, the kind of measure determines not only the size of the middle class in a particular country, but also its ranking relative to other countries. In a study by the Asian Development Bank, Malaysia ranked second in absolute terms, only 9th under the 75–125 per cent of the median expenditures of developing Asia, and 18th under the 75–125 per cent of the median expenditures of its country. As a result, the measures may change the assessment regarding which countries have a sizable middle class and how attractive a market will be for a company.

There is simply no single best measure: which measure you use should depend on your purpose and objective. If you are concerned about the economic and social structure of a country, for example, inequality, or the development of a country over time, irrespective of its rank in relation to others, you should use income distributions and distribution shapes over time, and comparisons to the poverty line. However, if you are focused on new consumers and the different markets, then an absolute measure that can be easily used to compare across markets will be the most practical measure. Of course, it makes a difference whether you define the middle class in terms of USD 2/USD 10 or USD 10/USD 100 because it may mean the difference between having just a roof over your head or living in an apartment, between using a tuk-tuk or bicycle, or owning a motorbike or car; between cooking your food over an open fire or preparing it in a kitchen. You need to be clear how exactly you draw the line. So, that decision should be determined by the products you produce and sell in a market.

The purchasing power of the Asian middle class

If we define the middle class as people earning between USD 2 and USD 20 a day, the total annual expenditures of Asia's middle class account for roughly 23 per cent of all global expenditures today. If we assume that there will be continued decreases in poverty within the Asia region, the Asian middle class may constitute the majority of purchasing power globally in the future.

For example, the Brookings Institution predicts that there will be a surge in the global middle class from roughly 6.8 billion in 2010 to 8 billion of the world population by 2030. More importantly, there will be a crossover of this group from the West to the East. Over the next 20 years, the global percentage of middle-class consumers in North America will decrease from 18 per cent to 7 per cent and in Europe from 36 per cent to 14 per cent, but it will increase in the Asia-Pacific from 28 per cent to 66 per cent.

Thus by 2030, in terms of consumption power, 59 per cent will be contributed by the Asia-Pacific, roughly twice the predicted share of consumption of North America and Europe combined. Moreover, the Brookings Institution predicts that over 70 per cent of China's population could be middle class (up from 12 per cent today), consuming USD 10 trillion in goods and services. And they are surprisingly optimistic about India, suggesting that "India could be the world's largest middle-class consumer market by 2030." The conclusion: "China and India are at the forefront of the expansion of the global middle class. The world economy can be expected to increasingly rely on the middle classes of these two Asian powers as key sources of global demand."

Young, trendy, online ... and everywhere

In a 2012 report titled "The Rise of the Middle Class in Asian Emerging Markets," KPMG identified some of the key characteristics of middle-class consumers in emerging Asian markets. First, the middle class in Asian emerging markets is made up of a younger population compared to their counterparts in the United States and Europe. For example, in India or in even a smaller market like Vietnam or Cambodia, more than 60 per cent of the population is under 30 years old, and they are or will be part of the middle class. Young middle-class consumers are particular about the brand and user experience. They will only stick to trusted and widely recognized brands. Second, the emerging middle classes in Asia emulate trends and like brands from developed markets such as the United States and Europe, and from developed Asian markets such as

Japan, South Korea, Hong Kong, and Singapore. The consumption of goods and services is more about enhancing one's self-identity and social status than it is about material satisfaction. Third, the emerging middle class is embracing online shopping. This new channel is gaining popularity fast through promotions on various social media platforms, blogs, and microblogs. Finally, the middle classes in Asian emerging markets are not only concentrated in the big cities. In China, middle-class consumer groups in smaller cities are growing at a faster rate than their counterparts in first-tier cities such as Beijing, Shanghai, and Guangzhou. In India, the middle classes are scattered around the country and are not concentrated only in cities such as New Delhi, Mumbai, and Bangalore.

Differences across countries

Over a 20-year period, from 1990 to 2010, the development of the Asian middle class has not been all the same across Asia, and would unlikely be so during the next 20 years. For example, the Brookings Institution's forecast about India may strike many as odd because India has lagged far behind China in the last 20 years. In China, the middle-class population has increased by approximately 850 million from 1990 to 2008, and resulted in an increase in total annual expenditures of USD 1.8 trillion. In contrast, although India has made progress in reducing the overall percentage of its poor and increasing the size of its middle class, low growth in per capita consumption has not outpaced population growth resulting in the addition of more than 84 million new poor people in 2008 as compared to 1990. In total, India has nearly 40 per cent of its people living below the global poverty line in both rural and urban areas.

Besides India, the Philippines, with about 20 per cent of its population living below the poverty line, is another country that has stagnated. Moreover, most of Indo-China (Cambodia, Laos, and Myanmar) has been left behind too. In 1997 *The New York Times* published an article, with a telling title, "In Cambodia, a Middleclassless Society." Only during the last few years a middle class seems to be emerging in Cambodia, primarily in the cities. Similar developments are taking place today in Laos. The Laotian youth are moving to the city of Vientiane and are keenly interested in the modern lifestyle and modern products (primarily, from neighboring Thailand). Finally, after years of military leadership, Myanmar, the last Asian country (besides North Korea) under autocratic rule, has opened up. Fifty years ago, Myanmar (then Burma) was one of Southeast Asia's leading economies; yet, in 2012 it had Southeast Asia's lowest per capita gross domestic product (GDP). Only one in four people has electricity, only 10 per cent have a bank account, and only 6 per cent have a mobile phone. A road network hardly exists. However, if Myanmar stays true to its reforms, economists predict that this frontier market could become a middle-class nation and more than triple its income by 2030.

Not much longer, maybe

Whereas some Asian countries seem to remain stuck in their development, China is steaming ahead. China has made great progress in the reduction of poverty. For example, it has decreased poverty so rapidly that this process has resulted in the creation of a middle class in most cities that is larger than that in the urban areas in the Philippines and similar to that in rural areas. This was achieved despite having started from a much more disadvantaged distribution (higher proportion of those living below the global poverty line) than the Philippines less than two decades ago.

Clearly, since it launched its open door policy, China seems to have gotten certain things right.

When I first visited China in 1991, the country was far behind other countries I saw in Asia; in comparison to China, the Philippines and Thailand seemed quite developed. Back then, China was roughly on par with India, at least in the cities. But China today is far ahead. Comparing Beijing with New Delhi, or Shanghai with Mumbai (or even a second-tier city in China with Mumbai) reveals a stark contrast. Chinese cities have modern infrastructures all across; Indian cities only at certain spots. Similarly when I visited the Philippines in 2012, and compared it to my first visit in the early 1990s, not much had changed. Everybody, though, was still saying that the big change will happen soon.

This does not mean that there are no problems and challenges in China. There is increased inequality. Corruption persists. China needs to define its identity (the political term for it is "Chinese dream"). There are also significant environmental problems. These are issues that China's new middle class is concerned about. However, other economies have gone through boom-and-bust periods and have developed much slower. As a result, their middle class, judging by economic indicators, does not seem to be as well-off. Government policies do matter, both for developing a middle class and protecting an existing middle class from being eroded. Governments in Asia should focus on continued improvements in education, health, and public services to improve disposable income, the quality of human capital, and the quality of life.

The professional middle class
The middle class is not only an economic phenomenon. Another way to define and analyze the middle class, favored by sociologists rather than economists, is by profession or standing within a society, and thus in terms of social class, status, and prestige. Having the

right mix of professions within a society can be as important as growing incomes.

The middle class dream

Historically, the earliest members of the middle class were the entrepreneurs and capitalists in Europe— the shopkeepers, traders, and bankers, as distinct from nobility. Since the industrial revolution, the term has been used to refer to managers and professionals, civil servants, scientists, engineers, doctors, teachers, and intellectuals—they formed the "middle" class between small farmers and the labor class on one side, and the landowners and capitalists on the other. Most of these middle-class professions are revered in Asia.

There has been a proud culture of successful traders in several Asian countries dating back to the British influence in the region; some countries have a tradition of confident civil servants as well as professionals and intellectuals. Teachers are highly respected in Asia, too. Cambodia, for example, lacks behind other Asian nations precisely because the middle class was targeted and largely extinguished between 1975 to 1979 under the Khmer Rouge regime, a radical communist movement that glorified peasant life.

Middle class lifestyle: coffee and movies

Finally, consumer behavior specialists consider the middle class as a unified consumption community characterized by what possessions its members have or strive for, by what they buy, and by how they buy. For example, once the basic needs for food and shelter are met, there is disposable income for consumer packaged goods (shampoos and detergents, cereals and snack foods, soft drinks and coffee), television sets, mobile phones, appliances, and cars. The middle class is also interested in credit cards, insurance, healthcare, and education for the next generation.

As income levels continue to rise, the middle class not only diversifies its spending but also demands better quality and innovation in the goods that they purchase. Middle-class consumers tend to switch consumption to more expensive items such as better tasting foods, or they may spend more time eating out. And there is differentiation in the products they use; for example, they do not wash their hands, clothing, and hair with the same piece of soap, but instead use different cleaning products (hand soap, detergent, shampoo). Moreover, middle class consumers love brands. They are committed to getting the right brand with the right image. They may become brand loyal. They flock to the shopping malls and shop online at e-commerce sites; they visit chat rooms and social networking sites to select and discuss their brand purchases. This drives competition amongst suppliers and presents the opportunity to target goods to specific segments and niches of consumers.

In other words, the middle class engages in a particular lifestyle. That's how Hong Kong's Financial Secretary, John Tsang, seems to regard the middle class. In 2013, he was quoted as saying that he understood well the worries of the middle class—being a member of it himself. He clarified his assessment by saying, "I have read articles that say the middle class are people who drink coffee and like

French movies. I like movies and tea, so there's not much difference (in my life) with the lives of the middle class." Indeed, the lifestyle of the Asian middle class is quite diverse.

The future of Asia's middle class

As the middle class in Asia is growing and changing, the size of the consumer pie is likely to be enlarged for both local enterprises and multinationals. It is important to understand, however, that Asia's rising middle class is diverse and constantly developing and changing. While local enterprises are challenged to keep consumers loyal to their brands rather than switching to international brands, as their needs and desires are changing, multinationals struggle with tailoring their products and services to suit local preferences. Also, for local and regional brands, the value added may be the in-depth knowledge of customer preferences and customer intimacy relative to price. For multinationals, value may be delivered through premium products where the value consists of perceived quality and image at a certain price point.

03

ASIAN PSYCHOLOGY
THE COLLECTIVIST MIND

Traditionally, Asians are part of cohesive in-groups. Nowadays they are becoming increasingly individualistic

What do we know about Asian culture and the Asian mind? How do Asians perceive the world, including products and brands? And how does their cultural mindset affect their behavior?

Such questions have been addressed in cross-cultural psychological research (comparing Westerners and Asians). This research has painted a picture of the unique characteristics of the Asian mind. Much of the work dates back to the seminal contributions of a Dutch social scientist, Geert Hofstede, who studied organizational culture and management. In his 1980 classic, *Culture's Consequences: International Differences in Work-related Values*, Hofstede defined culture along five different dimensions. He measured each dimension using respondents from different countries, and then conducted cross-country comparisons. Cultural dimensions theory, as we know it, was born.

The most widely studied of his five dimensions is individualism–collectivism. Hundreds of research studies have been conducted over the last 30 years on this dimension alone. Whereas Westerners and their cultures are seen as individualistic, Asians and their cultures, and societies, are seen as collectivist. Let's take a closer look at Asian collectivism.

Cohesion and the group
Hofstede proposed—and subsequent research largely supported his claim—that Asians are "integrated into strong, cohesive in-groups, often extended families (with uncles, aunts, and grandparents) who continue protecting them in exchange for unquestioning loyalty." Decisions are based on what is best for the group. There is a "we" and "us" mentality. The group has precedence over the individual. Because of group loyalty and a concern for harmony, people in collectivist societies avoid confrontation. An Asian individual may disagree with a person, but he or she would do so in private, and not in public, to protect a person from the "loss of face."

Collectivism has broad-based consequences at the national, political, and organizational levels. Political power belongs to interest groups. There is less social mobility. Organizations are often webs of extended families. Teachers and professors are held in high respect, and students are expected to sit still and listen to the wisdom of their teachers.

In collectivist societies, people also live closer to friends and family than in individualist societies. As a result, word of mouth and recommendations by friends and family are important when buying products. According to a survey of Chinese consumers published in the *McKinsey Quarterly* in 2013, only 53 per cent of Chinese found online recommendations credible but 93 per cent trusted recommendations from friends and family. The authors of the article recommend that companies may use word-of-mouth strategically to build a brand in a particular region. For example, the bottled water brand C'estbon has a small national market share in China, but a roughly 25 to 30 per cent market share on average in the southern part. Most of sales are to small stores and restaurants, where it has a dominant 45 to 50 per cent share in that region due to word-of-mouth. In India, the word-of-mouth approach resulted in success for P&G's brand of sanitary napkins, Whisper, which the company launched in targeted local communities.

Culture and the self

A collectivist culture creates a very different self and personality than an individualist culture. In one of the most widely cited articles in the social and behavioral sciences, psychologists Hazel Markus and Shinobu Kitayama drew a connection between culture and the self-identity of a person. They wrote that collectivism results in an "interdependent" rather than "independent" self-construal.

Self-construal is an individual's perception of himself or herself in a social context. An interdependent self-construal is defined as flexible and marked by sensitivity to situations and social contexts. The behavior of a person with an interdependent self-construal is contingent upon the feelings, thoughts, and behaviors of others. This results in a tendency of enacting appropriate behaviors, of fostering harmony with others, and of trying to fit in. Status, roles, relationships, and belongingness are central for the interdependent self. The concept of "face" is critical, and people act in accordance with the expectations of others rather than with their internal wishes or personal attributes.

As a result, when asked in marketing surveys, members of collectivist societies are more likely to say "yes" to interdependent self-construal statements such as "My relationships with those in my group are more important than my personal accomplishments;"

Group appeal in mass retail

"My happiness depends on the happiness of those in my group;" "I am careful to maintain harmony in my group;" and "I would sacrifice my self-interests for the benefit of my group." In contrast, they are less likely to agree with independent self-construal statements such as "My personal identity, independent of others, is very important to me" and "I enjoy being unique and different from others." As the title of one academic article put it so aptly: "I" value freedom, but "we" value relationships.

Brand positioning and luxury consumption

When companies position their products and brands, they should consider the Asian collectivist mind and its interdependent self-construal. In 2001, I collaborated with Jennifer Aaker, a professor at Stanford University, on a consumer experiment where we presented participants with two distinct kind of brand positioning—a "differentiation" positioning and an "assimilation" positioning.

Specifically, participants—Chinese and Americans—read the following instructions: "Timex watches is considering a new advertising campaign and is interested in getting feedback about it before the advertisements are created and the campaign is launched. Therefore, a very brief description of the central message in the advertising campaign will be given to you below, followed by a series of questions regarding your reactions to the campaign." Half of the participants saw a "differentiation positioning" for the brand. They were told that the central message was: "Timex watches. It embodies so much. It's like a person. It is an impressive personality, very individualistic, and with a strong focus and concern for oneself—in a positive way." In contrast, the other half saw an "assimilation positioning" where they read "Timex watches. It embodies so much. It's like a person. It is an impressive social being, very connected to others, and with a strong focus and concern for others—in a positive way." As expected, Chinese participants had higher preference for the brand in the assimilation positioning than the differentiation positioning, and vice versa for American participants.

The collectivist mind also affects luxury purchases. Nancy Wong, a professor at the Department of Consumer Science and Director of the Center for Retail Excellence at the University of Wisconsin at Madison, together with Aaron Ahuvia, conducts research on how self-construal affects consumption of luxury goods. She finds that "interdependent" Asian consumers tend to place great emphasis on publicly visible possessions and gravitate toward objects that display high social status. Professor Wong has an intriguing explanation for Asians' urge to splash on luxury goods. She argues that this reflects the importance of collectivism and conforming to the expectations of others. Conformity, in turn, fuels luxury expenditure through the concept of "face."

She explains that the Chinese concept of "face" has two aspects: *mein-tzu* is reputation based on success displayed ostentatiously, and *lien* refers to a person's basic moral worth in life. *Mien-tzu* can be enhanced by making enough money to build a lavish mansion, whereas *lien* can be enhanced by making charitable donations. In either case, it is a way to fit in by conforming to an in-group's ever-escalating expectations of acquiring possessions for socially appropriate appearance. Besides face, luxury consumption also results from another Asian collectivist phenomenon: the social obligations for gift-giving. Luxury gifts are recognized symbols to communicate esteem for the recipient and thus bring honor to the giver. In Asia, luxury consumption is therefore not necessarily tied to materialism; rather, it is sign of social virtue in fulfilling one's moral obligations.

The consumer research that I reviewed thus shows that collectivism influences brand positioning and luxury purchases. But how exactly are Asians collectivist and socially oriented toward others? For example, who is the "other" or the group that Asians decide to relate to?

To date, little research has gone into examining these issues. But I have a hunch based on years of observation. It seems to me that for the older generation, the family is the reference point. For young Asians, however, it is increasingly their friends. This is most pronounced among young Japanese and Koreans, but is also seen in India, Indonesia, and South Asia. As a result, Airtel, the world's third largest mobile communications company based in India, has positioned its brand with themes of friendship and sharing.

As a result, companies should pay close attention to nuances and intra-Asian variations in collectivism. When marketers design communications that feature groups and other individuals as role models, they should engage, for example, in detailed customer studies on how the collectivist mind and interdependent self-construal operate in a particular situation.

The individualistic consumer of the future

While collectivist influence is still predominant in Asian society, the young generation seems much more individualistic than the prior generation. Young consumers want to "express themselves" rather than "fit in." Take China. Due to its one-child policy and a rapidly developing consumer society, those "young emperors" grew up without siblings, and are therefore less socialized in a collectivist way. Moreover, parents who have only one child encourage independence and creativity rather than obedience and respect for others. Thus, child rearing, due to social policy, may prompt a profound change in the cultural values and behaviors in China.

This sets China apart from other Asian markets. But there are other reasons for the rise of individualism that are not specific to China, such as increased urbanization. Angela Lee, a consumer psychology professor at Northwestern University, and Ying Ding, a doctoral candidate at Peking University, have shown that teenagers from urban centers have independent self-construal whereas those from rural towns still have an interdependent self-construal.

In sum, businesses should consider the collectivist nature of Asians but be cautious in doing so. In the very near future, managers must consider the possibility that they may be dealing with far less collectivist, and more individualist and independently minded consumers in some markets. Moreover, aside from individualism–collectivism, it is about time to pay more attention to other cultural dimensions. Cultural psychologists Adam Cohen as well as C.Y. Chiu and Y.Y. Hong have noted that there many forms of culture and many constituents of culture (for example, religion, socioeconomic status, and region within a country; or material culture, the subjective culture of ideas and knowledge, and shared rules of social behavior). Psychologists and consumer researchers should study these additional dimensions of culture, which promise to provide new insights for managers in the future.

04

CONSUMER BEHAVIOR
WHAT MAKES ASIAN CONSUMERS TICK?

Asian shoppers display three seemingly contradictory desires. Smart companies bring it all together for them

When I browse online to find information about Asian consumers, or when I read the latest reports from agencies, I get confused. On the one hand, I read that Asian consumers are extremely concerned about price. They take a long time to decide, and they do not leave a store without receiving some sort of bargain—be it a discount or some goodies that they receive in conjunction with the purchase. On the other hand, I read about Asian consumers on shopping sprees—loaded with shopping bags, willing to spend uninhibitedly, and flashing their credit cards easily at the sales counter. They shop until they drop. I also read that Asian consumers are functionalists and think in practical terms. Yet, it often seems they just want to have fun and appear to be the most pleasure-seeking consumers in the world. Finally, I hear that Asians are traditionalists: they believe in conventional values and family, in Chinese medicine and Ayurveda, in ghosts and lucky numbers. They practice rituals and honor traditions. On the other hand, they seem to want to lead very contemporary lives. They seek out the latest fashions and engage in modern lifestyles. They seem to be oriented toward the future.

The postmodern Asian consumer

How can we make sense of these seemingly contradictory, even opposite behaviors? Are Asian consumers schizophrenic?

I don't think so. Rather, Asians seem to be "postmodern consumers" that can live with contradictions, in fact, they don't even view them as such. Confronted with a complex and fast changing world where multi-cultural traditions contrast with disruptive innovation, where the world of the countryside clashes with ultramodern cityscapes, where the familiar is undermined by global influences – in other words, a world where time and place are in constant flux and where identity needs to be constantly renegotiated and reconstructed – in such a world living with contradictions and embracing them seems the natural response. Keep in mind: the environmental conditions of the

"American consumer," when this consumer gained prominence after World War II, were entirely different: straight, linear, and familiar. As a result, the categories to describe the American consumer were clear and straightforward. This is not the case for the Asian consumer.

Asian consumers are multifaceted and drawn to both ends of the spectrum at the same time. They have diverse and bipolar desires. It is not a matter of segmenting them by one characteristic or the other, but understanding that they want many different things at the same time. This is the key insight that business leaders and marketers must understand, and base their strategies on.

More specifically, how do Asians choose products and brands? What are they looking for, and what matters to them. In other words, how do Asian buyers behave when they shop, what motivates them, and how do they perceive products and brands.

Behaviorally—when Asian consumers choose products and when they shop—they are looking for value; yet they also love to spend. Motivationally, they seem to seek and be driven by functionality and practicality; yet they want pleasure and fun as well. Finally, perceptually—that is, when it comes to the preferred image that they like in products and brands—Asians seem to prefer a unique combination of tradition and modernism, even futurism.

Value shopaholics

I am watching "Are Asians cheap?"—a short three-minute YouTube video produced by MyPanoo, an Asian teenager living in the United States. "No, we are not cheap," he starts out. The message, conveyed in the video in some combination of rap and slapstick, is "We are just smart … really smart. We like to save money ... After all, why do people like to spend? ... It's just a different way of thinking ... Many of us aren't rich and don't want to spend the money that we worked hard for … What if it was a compliment to say 'you are cheap'? What if it was seen as intelligent? Or as self control?" And so on.

Got the point, Panoo. There are other arguments one could add against the simplistic stereotype "Asians are cheap" notion. Asians just don't want to get ripped off and therefore often bargain. Plus, there is the collectivist nature of Asians that calls for honoring the prior generation's achievement of having worked hard to improve one's life, resulting in trying to make every cent count. It is not about not being spendthrift; it is about being frugal (*frugalis* in Latin means both thrifty and virtuous). Asians are smart in commercial settings and life. In a survey we conducted at ACI, called "The Pan-Asian WAVE Consumer Study," one of the key finding was that Asians are financially conservative. What they want when they shop is *value*. In sum, Asians are "value-driven consumers."

Perceived value is one of the most essential marketing concepts. Wikipedia defines it as follows:

> the difference between the prospective customer's evaluation of all the benefits and all the cost of an offering and the perceived alternatives ... It is often expressed as the equation: Value = Benefits/Cost.

The concept of perceived value may be interpreted broadly by considering not only the immediate costs and benefits related to a product purchase but also costs invested in having a certain amount of disposable income ("working hard"), and the psychological benefits received from being cost-conscious ("I am being smart").

However, while shopping for value, Asians are also compulsive shopaholics and love to spend. For example, with rising individualism, many second-generation consumers now lavishly spend the fortune that their parents have accumulated. According to a 2006 AC Nielsen study, the world's keenest "recreational shoppers" are found in Asia. In Singapore, where shopping is a national pastime, 90 per cent of consumers say they go shopping as a form of entertainment. For many, it is a weekly ritual. They live what I call a "mall lifestyle." To them a perfect shopping and lifestyle mall has all sorts of goods to buy, from fashion and accessories to home furnishings and cosmetics, and a range of services such as hair salons, spas, and movie theaters. A large food court is a must. The mall must have the latest international brands. Facilities should be clean and glitzy. Singaporeans usually visit malls in pairs and no more than four people. They often spend an entire day in the mall or hop from one mall to the next. It seems to be their idea of happiness. The only inconvenience that may interrupt the happy glow from shopping may be a five-minutes-late arrival of the public transport. Tell that story to a London shopper using the Tube!

You may think Singaporeans are extreme. Yet Hong Kong consumers, Thais, Koreans, and other Asians are not far behind. In terms of the proportion of people who go shopping at least once a week simply to occupy their time, seven of the top ten markets are in Asia. A third of Chinese consumers and one-fifth of Indians say shopping for clothes is their favorite thing to do. "For Asians,

Yes!!! Another mall.

shopping is retail therapy," my marketing colleague at Columbia Business School in New York, Leonard Lee, a Singaporean, tells me. "They feel good by shopping." Clearly, Professor Lee, who conducts research on shopping and retailing, has found a perfect subject of study in Asian consumers.

Internet shopping is also gaining popularity in Asian markets. The top three growth markets are South Korea, China, and India. While South Korea's internet economy is mature, contributing already 8 per cent to its GDP, China and India are smaller markets in relative terms but fast growing. In the period

Seeking pleasure and performance

from 2010 to 2016, India is predicted to have a compound annual growth rate for its internet economy of 23 per cent and China of 17 per cent. South Korea, China, and India also stand out for their enormous internet-related exports—South Korea overall, China in goods, India in services. In China, consumer-to-consumer e-commerce is popular; Taobao, where consumers sell to each other, transacted more merchandise in 2010 than the country's top five brick-and-mortar retailers combined.

But the shopping obsession is paired with price sensitivity. Whether they shop online or in stores, Asian consumers are looking for "a deal." Getting a bargain is a way to feel good. They want value. In sum, Asian consumers are "value shopaholics."

Functional hedonists

Motivationally, Asians are often described as functionalists. They are looking for practicality and utility in products. The reason for this is the engineering mentality in the region. Engineers are revered because they produce tangible value. Asian consumers are drawn to well-engineered technology products. Asians with smartphones in their hands or playing with the latest tech gadgets have become one of the iconic images of modern commercial life.

Asians are also analytically minded. Keep in mind that this is the part of the world where students achieve the highest math test scores. Asians are analytical as consumers as well, examining closely the features and benefits of products before making a choice.

At the same time, Asians are hedonists as well. For them, consumption counts as a justifiable means of getting pleasure. There is also a close link between hedonism and experiences. Experiences provide the entertainment, enjoyment, and fun that hedonists are seeking.

For example, Asian women obsessively follow trends in the fashion industry and wear the latest styles. They love to hear about fashion trends and discuss them feverishly with their friends. Asian women are extremely interested in beauty products. Their closets are stacked to the top with skincare and cosmetics. The beauty routine of Asian women is far more extensive than that of Western women. Some markets, like Korea, are leading the world in redefining beauty through technologies such as plastic surgery.

In sum, again, it seems that Asians are motivated by two seemingly incompatible desires: to gain functionality, and at the same time, to enjoy pleasure and positive emotions from products. Asian consumers are "functional hedonists."

Traditional futurists

Finally, Asians are considered to be traditionalists and to be influenced by long-lasting societal norms and conventions. These traditions are tied to philosophical, religious, or spiritual value systems such as Buddhism, Hinduism, Confucianism, and Taoism. These broad-based systems affect individual perceptions of the relations between body and mind, food and health, lifestyle and beauty, and in turn, exercise subtle influences on consumer perceptions of food and beauty products.

For example, the Chinese subscribe to a wide set of beliefs about the longevity and vigor of certain food ingredients. Certain foods and drinks are supposed to be avoided when one experiences yin or yang deficiency. The symbolic meanings of food at Chinese New Year celebrations are extensive: abalone offers good fortune; bamboo fungus offers a long life; bean curd sticks bless the house; eggs promise fertility; glass noodles symbolize long life; lychee is associated with close family ties; oysters mean good business; pomegranate means many offspring; water chestnut symbolizes unity, just to name a few. These associations are based on superficial similarities (e.g., eggs and fertility; pomegranate and offspring) or on linguistic play (e.g., homonyms that share identical pronunciations for the food item and abstract concept), and are not really supposed to be taken that seriously. Yet the Chinese take them seriously, although I still have to figure out whether they are merely repeating some habit or tradition, or whether they seriously believe the symbolic meanings.

Asians hold auspicious beliefs not only about food but also about other aspects of their lives. In 2012 (on Friday, the 13th of April, an unlucky day by the Western calendar), the Institute on Asian Consumer Insight (ACI) that I am directing in Singapore organized an event titled "Ghost, Lucky Numbers, and Other Superstitions, and How They Influence Consumer Behavior" with an Asian industry panel that focused on superstitions beliefs and practices from their different businesses. They provided examples and debated how superstitious beliefs affect the buying and decision making of Chinese, Indian, Korean, and Indonesian consumers. Examples include specific feng shui placements of furniture equating "good luck" and how lucky or unlucky numbers may affect wealth and profits in business. These superstitious beliefs are particularly significant for the retail and property sectors. While their validity is questionable, they nonetheless serve important psychological functions. In a rapidly modernizing world, many things may seem beyond our control. As such, our fundamental human need for control drives us to seek patterns and connections in the world to help us make sense of the uncertainty in our own lives. This need is conveniently filled by these cultural beliefs.

However, Asians, especially city-dwellers, are also highly future-focused and innovation-oriented. As a result, traditions and culture (in the sense of dress codes, language, and physical culture) are becoming less important. Traditional dress codes hardly exist any longer: when did you last see a Japanese woman in a kimono, a Chinese woman in a qipao, or a Southeast Asian woman in a sarong? You still see Indian and Pakistani women in saris, but rarely young women. Such outfits are reserved for cultural ceremonies and festivals, or flight attendant uniforms (think: Singapore Airlines). In modern society, they play a minor role at best. Also, in business, English has become the common language, and Chinese may become the language of the future. Asian cities are increasingly characterized by uniform modern cityscapes. Traditional buildings are disappearing quickly, replaced by faceless apartment complexes and highways or ultramodern buildings by international star architects.

Again, Asians unite seemingly incompatible opposites. They yearn for anchors from the past and for traditions. But they also want to live in the future. Asian consumers are "traditional futurists."

Postmodern brands will thrive

What kind of brands might Asians with seemingly contradictory desires find most attractive? Probably those that transcend linear positioning, such as postmodern brands that deconstruct complex, seemingly incompatible imagery and present it in an integrative way.

These postmodern brands are particularly attractive to Asians because they unite the opposite trends that I have discussed in

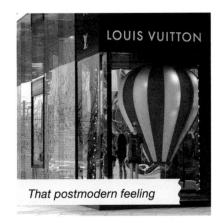

That postmodern feeling

this chapter. Consider Louis Vuitton. Although the brand has a long history, it does not come across as stuffy. Rather, it has launch edgy new products such as, in 2003 the colorful bag designed by Japanese designer and artist Takashi Murakami. The bag itself nicely incorporates high and low art into the merchandise. It is functional but also a hedonic treat. It uses the traditional LV logo (from 1896) but deconstructs it in a futuristic way. At roughly USD 2000 it is affordable for the new upper-middle class lifestyle consumer and the perfect handbag for female value shopaholics. Not surprisingly, it was a runaway success in Asia.

Another feature of postmodern brands is their close association with popular culture. "The heroes of postmodernism tend to be celebrities and entertainment figures whose taste and consumption habits are held as models for us all," writes Arthur Asa Berger, a media expert. In ACI's Pan-Asian WAVE Consumer Study we found evidence for it. Asian consumers, particularly Indians (perhaps because of the prominence of Bollywood), adore celebrities and are likely to choose brands promoted by them. Similar admirations of celebrities and popular culture can be observed in many Asian cities including Hong Kong, Shanghai and Taipei. Therefore to appeal to Asia's postmodern consumers, it is critical to connect a brand to popular culture and entertainment.

05

METHODOLOGY
HOW TO GAIN CONSUMER INSIGHT

Collecting and analyzing data to gain insight is both a research and organizational challenge

Decision makers know that consumer insight is essential for developing strategies on Asian markets and implementing these strategies in new product development, selling, and communications. They are aware that a new, unprecedented insight into a key target group of Asian consumers could be worth a fortune.

As a result, market research agencies and consumer research departments within organizations have renamed and rebranded themselves as "consumer insight agencies" or "consumer insight departments." The term "consumer insight" has become a buzzword.

Analysis and creativity

Insight, taken seriously, is more than market and consumer research. Such research may be a starting point, but it takes knowledge, intuition, and experience to translate data into intelligence that results in innovative and actionable strategies and implementations. Real insight leads to an "epiphany"—when a previously intractable problem is suddenly understood. Real insight is about connecting the dots in new ways, and seeing new connections, new relations, and new applications. It thrives as much on creativity as it requires scientific data analyses.

Decision makers are often confused by the multitude of insight methodologies and the hype surrounding some of the techniques that researchers are using. Some have been around for decades; others are fairly new. Some are verbal; others are observational. Some are quantitative; others are qualitative. It can be quite confusing. Let me first sort these techniques out for you as a manager. I will then examine how data gained from these techniques can be used for gathering true insights.

Traditional research techniques

Many traditional techniques such as focus groups, one-on-one interviews, and surveys are verbal in nature. They have been used for decades. Depending on the research purpose, they are also still useful today. At ACI in Singapore, we have used these methodologies in various projects. We have run focus groups with consumers from different nations, conducted expert interviews across Asia, and commissioned a large-scale survey called "Pan-Asian WAVE Consumer Study," which polled 7,000 consumers in 10 Asian markets to examine consumer needs, values, priorities and beliefs.

The focus group is a qualitative research technique where a skilled moderator (or two) asks consumers a series of questions about their perceptions, attitudes, and behaviors. The method usually includes a small group of consumers (between 8 and 12). The moderator must show respect and empathy for the participants, and most importantly, keep the group discussion focused on the key issues. A moderator must also be well prepared and ready to act spontaneously when he or she feels an insightful point is being made. As an exploratory research technique, a focus group will not result in final answers. It is also hardly representative of a larger population, or even a specific target group. But it is a first step that can lead to preliminary insight that may be further tested with other research techniques.

When conducting focus groups in Asia, moderators should be aware of potential problems. It is important to watch out for the right mix of males and females in the group, and to take note of the cultural and ethnic backgrounds of the participants. The moderator must also be sensitive to what is called "power distance"—the obligation of a younger person or a person of lower rank to be deferential toward elders or superiors. It may be considered rude to disagree with an older or more senior person. Another problem with conducting focus groups in Asia is that Asians may be concerned about sharing their opinions because of how they are being perceived by others. They do not want to lose face in front of others or the moderator. That is what the research on running focus groups in Asia says.

The problem of "face" also occurs when conducting interviews. As in the case of focus groups, Asian interviewees may be hesitant to share their opinions for fear of losing face in front of the interviewer. However, my own experience of observing focus groups and interviews in Asia has convinced me that these issues are much less of a concern when doing research among young Asians. The young generation is quite individualistic; they can be talkative and eager to share their opinions. The challenge with them is to keep them focused and on track, both in focus groups and interviews.

How about surveys? Conducting surveys can help overcome the sampling shortcomings and concerns for lack of reliability of focus groups and interviews. Surveys are administered to larger samples of consumers and they are more structured, and thus more conclusive. Yet, running a survey study is a science; so I highly recommend outsourcing a survey to an agency to marketing research experts. There are too many details to watch out for and only an experienced firm can do a good job. For instance, there are a variety of sampling techniques, question formats, and statistical analyses that are essential in conducting a reliable and valid survey study. Many surveys nowadays are web-based. Moreover, as with focus groups and interviews, there are specific sampling issues and response biases to consider and correct for when conducting surveys in Asia, such as respondents' tendency to agree and not to use extreme responses.

IdeaBlast™

At ACI, we have developed IdeaBlast™ as an alternative to existing methods such as focus groups, interviews and surveys. Focus groups, interviews, and surveys may be valid research techniques, but they rarely produce real insight. More than that: they are rarely useful for new idea generation and new product development. They often provide you with a consensus opinion and with information that you know already. Ask yourself: Did you ever get a "big idea" out of a focus group or interview? Do these research techniques help you create disruptive innovations or really new products? Have these methods resulted in customer insight that truly differentiates you from competitors?

In focus groups, there are moderators who listen carefully but rarely ask provocative questions. Most interviewers follow interview guidelines and don't probe deeply for insight. Survey questions are tested over and again for their reliability, but rarely for their practical relevance. Responses are limited to selecting options rather than voicing opinions. As a result, many participants provide cut-and-dried, analytical responses that don't get under their skin.

IdeaBlast™ is different. The IdeaBlast™ sessions that we conduct at ACI may involve one-on-one exchanges with sharp experts, or we bring together a diverse, articulate, and passionate group of consumers. We intentionally shake up and provoke consumers so that they reveal their true feelings, motivations, and desires. We strive for primal reactions from participants, rather than well-thought out, but standard responses. Our moderators and interviewers act as provocateurs who take positions and ask consumers to react. And the output of our IdeaBlast™ sessions is not an easily digested research report. Instead, we provide our clients with three simple "big ideas" and a summary of provocative statements obtained from the participants.

Observations and brain machines

Experts in the industry have pointed out several drawbacks to verbal research techniques. Respondents may be self-conscious; they may have difficulties verbalizing how they feel; or they may simply lie. Observational techniques avoid these problems because they record consumers' behavior or automatic reactions, rather than their attitudes or opinions, or verbalized introspections about their feelings and shopping habits.

Conventional observations of outside behavior are done in commercial settings—on shopping streets, or outside and inside stores. Observers unobtrusively take note of consumer behavior in real time, with or without a scoring sheet. In my course on Asian consumer insight, I have sent students to shopping malls to observe how shoppers behave in such malls and inside stores.

A more recent and much more expensive technique is brain scanning. Neuroscientists use brain scanning techniques, such as fMRI, to create a topography of the brain that displays which part of the brain is responsible for which function. Consumer neuroscientists, by observing hope to get unbias consumer insights.

I have co-authored a consumer neuropsychology study using functional magnetic resonance imaging (fMRI) and have had a full body scan myself. It is no fun to be in these machines; you may feel claustrophobic, and the noise inside the machine is deafening. As a result, in a given study, there are usually only a very small number of respondents who are included in the study (about ten). And they are often shown only very simple stimuli (in our own study we showed participants just the logos of various brands).

Unfortunately, even simple perceptual and cognitive functions (such as recognizing the shape of a logo) are widely distributed across the brain. Matters are far more complicated for complex cognitive functions and behaviors such as recalling a brand name, forming a judgment about a product, or making a choice among alternatives. That makes things difficult for marketers and consumer behaviorists because we would like to find out what it means when one area of the brain rather than another is activated in an fMRI scan. The simple answer is, in most circumstances, we just don't know.

Despite all the hype, neuroscience studies are, in my view, of limited use in marketing. Moreover, it is questionable whether brain scanning studies can tell us anything about the similarities and differences among Asian consumers. The brain is the result of tens of thousands of years of evolution; it is extremely unlikely to see practically differences among Asians, or even between Asians and Westerners, reflected in differential brain activities.

Ethnography and big data

There are two other research techniques that are currently "hot" in consumer insight circles: ethnography and big data.

Ethnography examines the system of meanings in the life of a cultural group. Applying methods from the fields of ethnology and anthropology, consumer ethnographers spend time with Asian consumers (usually from one to several days) to observe and study their daily practices in order to understand their living conditions and habits. What the researcher is hoping to gain is to find the pearl of consumer insight that can be translated ultimately into a successful product that adds value to the consumer. Ethnography is frequently done as field research, often in rural settings in emerging markets to study issues such as privacy, personal hygiene, or community relations. In the future, especially in Asia, ethnography may be supplemented by data collected via smartphones, which can also track consumer behaviors as they occur as part of people's daily lives.

My ACI colleague Julian Cayla writes that ethnographic stories provide executives with a new way of understanding market realities. In my course on Asian consumer insight, I ask my students to gain an in-depth understanding of an Asian consumer by shadowing the consumer and immersing themselves deeply into his or her life and lifestyle. Students are told to observe and ask questions about the consumer's private life, lifestyle, life as a shopper, and influences on the consumer's behavior. They are supposed to observe without intruding or directing. They may ask probing questions but must be respectful when doing so. Most importantly, they should try to see the world from the consumer's perspective. In their final presentation to me, they are supposed to go beyond the data by presenting one key insight about the consumer they observed and providing supporting evidence for the insight. To support their insight, they can provide quotes, present a profile of the consumer, and show pictures or a video of the consumer's daily life or shopping habits. The results are often impressive: most students provide a sharp understanding of what makes that consumer tick and generate insightful ideas about how to market to this consumer.

The opposite technique to the deep dive of ethnography is the analysis of massive data sets, of millions of observations, referred to as "big data." The rise of big data is fueled by the increasing volume of information captured by organizations through media and the internet. There will be exponential growth in data for the foreseeable future. Data will mostly be in the form of numbers but may also include textual and visual elements for which new data analytic techniques are currently being developed.

The new world of big data raises issues of how to collect and keep such data in a data warehouse, and how to analyze them to capture insights ("data analytics"). Big data can be used for all sorts of decisions, from segmentation of consumers to new product development and service applications. They can be a key source of competitive advantage. The key issue and challenge of big data, as with other research techniques, is how to turn the raw data into insight.

Turning data into insight

Any research technique – whether it is data analytics, ethnography and observations, or verbal research techniques – can be a source of competitive advantage only if it result in unique, actionable insights that are, in fact, acted on. Senior managers I talk to frequently complain that their research departments flood them with data, findings, and statistics that contain little insight, and little concern for the decision issues at hand. As a result, senior management often ignores the data and goes by gut instinct. Or they use the data from the insight department to justify previously made decisions. I don't blame them. Senior management feels frustrated because insight departments behave like academics or technocrats: they blindly follow procedures and are more concerned about the accuracy of their findings than whether these findings are relevant and useful.

To better understand the needs of decision makers, the data collectors, researchers and analysts (that is, "the insight teams") should work closely with management. Insight teams may then be able to provide more relevant inputs and make more useful contributions to key decisions. That is, insight specialists must be willing to frame their research in managerial and actionable terms by focusing on essential analyses rather than getting caught up, and obsessed with, floods of information in quantitative and qualitative data. There needs to be an open communication and exchange between insight teams and management decision makers. Both must be willing to understand each other's role and function, and accommodate them into their areas of expertise in order to achieve jointly the best business results and outcomes.

ASIAN ST

In section 2, I will present strategies and tools for managing your business in Asia. I will show you how to make Asian consumers a strategic priority, how to segment markets, how to build brands – and more.

Let's plan your next move and a lon term strategy for your business.

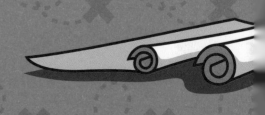

Business and marketing strategy is about planning for achieving desirable goals in the future. Part of successful strategic planning is having a certain mindset and determination. I will first show that you must define Asian consumers as your key priority to succeed in the region.

Asian markets are diverse. At the broadest level of strategy, executive decision makers need to ask themselves a key question: which level of the market should they focus on: the bottom, the middle, or the top of the market? For most companies, the answer will be rightly the middle class; however, the middle class itself is quite broad and fraught with its own challenges and obstacles.

Is it possible to embark on a standardized, pan-Asian strategy? I will address the perennial issue of standardization and localization. I will conclude that companies err too much on the side of localization. A localization approach seems customer-focused and culturally sensitive, but extreme localization provides too detailed of a cut to be useful for implementation.

Given the increased importance of branding, I will also make recommendations for brand strategy.

How should you position your brand? What kind of brands are Asians attracted to? How important is the brand experience relative to the performance characteristics of the brand?

Finally, I will share with you five strategic tools that I have developed for ACI—the new Institute on Asian Consumer Insight in Singapore. At ACI, we have used these tools in our work with multinational corporations as well as with regional and local clients. The case examples I am providing in this section are similar, but not identical, to some of the client projects that we have done.

The portfolio of strategy and analysis maps and tools that I will feature include

(1) *the Asia Strategy Map*™ (for plotting a long-term roadmap for your business);

(2) *the Concept Exploration Method*™ (for discovering new market opportunities);

(3) the Asian Lifestyle Tool™ (for designing customized products and services);

(4) The Brand Experience Wheel™ (for transforming a functional brand into an experience);

(5) *the Online-Offline Mix Metrics™* (for investing in an effective omni-channel strategy).

06

FOCUS ON ASIA
MAKING ASIAN CONSUMERS A PRIORITY

As Asia is moving from a supplier to a consumer market, companies need to make Asian consumers a priority to succeed

How do you view Asia and its consumers? Are you still adopting what I call a "wait-and-see" attitude towards Asian consumers? Or are you rather proactive about them, or view them even as a strategic priority? In other words, what is your strategic stance toward Asian consumers?

The term "strategic stances" is a common concept in the strategy literature. It was introduced in the pioneering work of Charles Miles and Charles Snow *Organizational Strategy, Structure, and Process,* one of the most influential and highly cited strategy and management books. The term refers to the overall attitude, or mental frame, that firms assume toward a particular market and its consumers, and how they structure their organization accordingly. Depending on your strategic stance toward Asian markets and consumers, your organization will be structured, and act, quite differently.

Wait-and-see is a passive and reactive approach. It is about reacting to a market after finding out for the first time that there may be a potential—that is, that a market may be ready for your products. Adopting a proactive stance means believing that a market clearly exists and acting accordingly. Making Asian markets and consumers a top strategic priority for your firm means that Asia may take precedence over some other markets. Asia consumers will be viewed as a leading market of global importance for your business because you consider them essential for the future growth of your company.

Who cares about Asian consumers?

For most of the 20th century, Asian markets and its consumers were not a priority, nor actively pursued by many companies. There wasn't even much of a wait-and-see attitude. Asian consumers were of minor interest to many firms from outside the region, and even firms within the region focused largely on manufacturing. Most of Asia was a supplier: a supplier of components (such as Taiwan), or cheap labor (for example, China and Vietnam for apparel), or a supplier of services (think of the programming and technology personel from India). Asia was the world's factory—a place where components or products were produced on the cheap and assembled. The finished products and brands were then exported, and sold in the West. A brand name was stuck onto the finished products and a premium price charged for the brands.

This was the common way of doing business. Within Asia, after World War II, Japanese companies were the first to seize the opportunity of manufacturing on the cheap in Asia, similar to Western firms, and then exporting its products to the West. In the 1960s and 1970s, the country industrialized quickly and became a developed economy that exported its products (primarily consumer electronics and cars) to the West. In the 1970s and 1980s, the four Asian Tigers (South Korea, Taiwan, Hong Kong, and Singapore) followed Japan's lead in developing an export-oriented economy and became the so-called "newly industrialized economies." From the 1990s to the first decade of the 21st century, China's open door reforms transformed the country and Asia as a whole. Before Deng Xiao Peng's open door policy in 1979, China was not on the map of any Western or many Asian companies. It was seen as a backward, communist state not interested in foreign investment. Soon after the open door policy began, Western firms reacted to the new circumstances and shifted manufacturing to China. After China came India and Vietnam. Over time in the 1990s and 2000s, Asia has been gradually moving toward the center of the world economic stage. Now it enjoys rapid GDP growth, strong foreign exchange reserves, and a competitive manufacturing industry. It has weathered the world financial crisis in the second part of the first decade of the new millennium quite well. Most importantly, Asia's growing consumer markets are finally of keen interest to most firms because these consumer markets present new business opportunities for growth and expansion.

From supplier to consumer markets

The shift from viewing Asia as a supplier and manufacturing base toward focusing on Asian consumers marks a major turn in terms of strategic thinking about Asia.

Many companies nowadays feel most Asian markets are worth the risk. Asia has become a vital and strategic market for companies to remain globally competitive, and they have adjusted their organizations and operations accordingly.

Initially, Western firms and Japan, and then Korea, took a wait-and-see stance, dedicating minimal resources to the new Asian markets. Here was a new export market where one could sell what had already been made. There was no need to change products, nor to alter or customize them. There were no specific products for Asian markets *per se*. Organizationally, everything was controlled from the headquarters. However, once firms adopted a proactive stance, they saw opportunities in Asian markets. They began asking whether products may need to be modified to be successful. They increased their investments and spent more resources—in people, in customer insight teams, in marketing and sales. Now, as some companies view Asia as a key priority, they are moving research and development (R&D) into the region. They are sending top personnel to the region and are giving them a say in global decisions. They launch new products just for the region or first in the region for world markets; they focus on brand building and service quality; and they relocate innovation activities to Asia. They are also establishing regional headquarters in Asia, and they have Asians run these operations.

Over the years, firms have also changed their foreign market entry mode in Asia. In the beginning, it was all about exporting rather than foreign direct investment. After gaining some knowledge and experience in the host country, companies may have expanded their operations in that country through ownership of production or distribution facilities. This incremental approach allowed a firm to get a grip on Asia without major investment. Nowadays, in many Asian markets, firms use a combination of various foreign direct investments, including wholly owned subsidiaries, joint ventures, and strategic alliances. In contrast to exporting, foreign direct investment offers more control and higher profit returns. However, it carries higher risks and is organizationally more complex.

When a company has decided that Asia is a critical growth and revenue market for its products and services, and that Asian consumers constitute a strategic priority then it must make certain choices and ask itself a series of key strategic questions. First, which level of the market should it target—the large population of poor consumers in Asian emerging markets, or the middle class, or perhaps the small but growing group of affluent consumers? Second, how should it segment the market? Can it pursue a pan-Asian strategy, or does it have to pursue regional or local strategies? And how about its branding and positioning strategy? Should it position its brands as international or local, as quality, as prestige, or as an experience?

Such strategic choices are of critical importance for market success. Answers to these questions depend on a multitude of factors: the stage of development of a market, the product category and brands, the competition, and the consumer. The questions must be addressed with knowledge about Asian consumers and markets, and the right strategy tools. Most importantly, these strategies must be flexible and adaptive to the ever-changing market conditions of hyper-dynamic Asian markets.

07

CONSUMER TARGETING
WHO SHOULD YOU TARGET?

The bottom, the middle and the top of the market may seem attractive. However, most fortune, now and in the future, will be made with the middle class

Using a simple model, we can distinguish three broad consumer segments in Asian markets: the poor, the middle class, and the affluent. They differ drastically. So, who should we focus on and target? The poor who barely participate as consumers in the marketplace, the middle class with its endless appetite for new products and brands, or wealthy consumers engaged in lifestyle and luxury consumption?

Silly question—but wait ...

For most businesses, this sounds like a silly question. The answer seems obvious: the middle class, of course. The major concern of the poor at the bottom is survival rather than consumption; they are a large group of billions of potential consumers, but they have little purchasing power. The rich at the top, on the other hand, seem to be too small a group in size to be lucrative for many businesses.

Yet some disagree. These dissenters are associated with the so-called "Bottom of the Pyramid" (BoP) movement. One of the pioneers of the BoP movement was the late C.K. Prahalad, a prominent management strategist of Indian origin, who taught at the University of Michigan. Prahalad presented his radical views in a 2004 book titled *Fortune at the Bottom of the Pyramid: Eradicating Poverty through Profits*. He argued that companies have ignored the untapped purchasing power at the bottom of the pyramid. Companies can make significant profits by selling to the poor, and large multinational companies should play the leading role in this process. By doing so, they can bring prosperity to the poor and help eradicate poverty.

The BoP concept is very popular, especially in India where numerous conferences have been held to debate the concept. Yet, there are some serious problems with the BoP position. Anil Karnani, a colleague of C.K. Prahalad at the University of Michigan, laid them out. He finds Prahalad's proposition that selling to the poor can simultaneously be profitable and eradicate poverty appealing, but too good to be true. "It is seductively appealing, but it is riddled with fallacies. There is little glory or fortune at the bottom of the pyramid—unfortunately, it is (almost) all a mirage," he writes.

Huge population, limited market

First, Professor Karnani argued that C.K. Prahalad vastly overestimated the market size at the bottom of the pyramid. While the population is huge, the actual global market is quite small (less than USD 0.3 trillion, compared to the USD 11 trillion economy in the United States alone). Second, virtually none of the examples cited by BoP proponents support the proposition that companies can make a fortune by selling to the poor. The costs associated with serving the markets at the bottom of the pyramid can be very high, and the poor are often geographically dispersed and culturally heterogeneous (except for the urban poor living in slums). The dispersion of the poor in the countryside increases distribution and marketing costs, and makes it difficult to achieve economies of scale. Weak infrastructures (transportation, communication, media, and legal) further increase the cost of doing business. Finally, another factor leading to high costs is the small size of each transaction. Because of that, many companies pursuing a BoP strategy keep the unit cost high. Professor Karnani concludes:

Private companies should try to market to the poor. However, the profit opportunities are modest at best and I suggest a cautious approach. Large companies that require scale economies should be even more hesitant. The best opportunities exist when the firm reduces price significantly by innovatively changing the price-quality trade-off in a manner acceptable to the poor.

He proposes an alternative perspective on how the private sector can help alleviate poverty. Rather than viewing the poor primarily as consumers, an alternative approach is to empower them as producers and emphasize buying from them, thus creating new markets among poor consumers.

Arunachalam Muruganantham, who says he comes from a "below poverty line" family, followed this approach in his quest to produce an affordable sanitary napkin that village women in India could use during menstruation. He had noticed that his wife had used dirty rags in their home because buying sanitary napkins were too expensive. If she had bought them, she wouldn't have been able to afford milk for the family then. The napkins he invented were made on simple machines in rural parts of India. He gave away many of these machines rather than going into mass production. The local model of production is low-tech and decentralized, providing opportunities for women to form cooperatives and generate some income. The napkins are sold under the label Laadli ("Beloved Daughter") for about 10 rupees whereas Procter & Gamble sells napkins for 30 rupees.

In a similar vein, Vision Spring, a social enterprise that distributes affordable eye glasses, was launched in India in 2005. The organization uses the income generated from a high-volume, low-margin approach to bring eyecare to BoP consumers living in remote locations. They trained local people, so-called "vision entrepreneurs" to give eye screenings and sell eyeglasses. Vision Spring is, however, not really a commercial success; it is also dependent on charity. Procter & Gamble, incidentally, engaged in its own BoP efforts, developing a chemical treatment called PUR that converts contaminated water into drinking water. As a commercial project, PUR was a failure. But the positive result was that, a while later, the company provided packets of PUR to relief efforts and nonprofits—a philanthropic, community-based approach that has been far more successful.

In sum, commercial success at the bottom of the pyramid is questionable. What seems to work in some circumstances, however, is a community-based philanthropic approach that helps BoP communities to become entrepreneurial and take care of themselves.

Any luck at the top?

So, if the fortune to be gained at the bottom of the pyramid is limited, how about the top? According to a report issued in 2012 by Capgemini consultancy and RBC Wealth Management, the Asia-Pacific Region now has for the first time ever more individuals with more than USD 1 million in investable assets than North America (a total of 3.7 million). Aren't the rich in Asia grabbing luxury good after luxury good, high-end designer brands, high-end cars, and premium properties?

The problem is that while the market is profitable, consumers at the top know exactly what they want, and it is usually a few high-end established brands with a legacy. Thus, you either have it or you don't because it would take years to develop the quality products that they are interested in and even longer to build the brand. This will be a challenge for Asian firms, in particular. Foreign firms, such as Italian, French, American, or German luxury brands selling furniture, fashion, jewelry, cars, or yachts, have the traditional image that these consumers desire. In Asia, at the top end of the market, tradition sells. Yet, Asians will not easily fall for newly created brands. They look for history and legacy, and the labels for it (e.g., "founded in," *"depuis,"* and *"seit"*).

Back to the middle class

Thus, the right target for most companies seems to be the middle class. The middle class, however, is fraught with its own challenges. First, it is diverse and constantly changing; it is far less uniform in its specific preferences and choices than the classes below and above it, and it is different from its Western counterparts. By income alone, we can distinguish three diverse groups. First, there are the middle-class consumers who only recently entered the middle class (call them the "lower middle class"). They are first-time consumers of basic consumer electronics and household appliances and fast-moving consumer goods. Then there is the core of the middle class—motivated to stabilize their status, upgrading their first-generation products, and becoming brand aware and loyal to certain brands. Finally, there is the "upper middle class," consuming a much wider variety of goods and services, engaging in conspicuous consumption, oriented toward the upper classes, and eager to move further up.

Some argue that it is misleading to talk about the middle class in Asia as one consumer segment (or even three) that can be targeted with a middle-class strategy. Instead, there may be many consumption-specific middle-class segments across Asia with different interests and desires. If we focus on product features alone, we will see that there are some who seek functionality; there are others who seek style and design; and there are those who like to show off their newly acquired status. In other words, what those companies that focus on the middle class really need is a brand portfolio that targets value and lifestyle segments rather than the middle class as a whole or by income categories. They need to develop a pipeline of products, services, and brands that can serve middle-class lifestyle desires at every level. This is quite a challenge!

The future of Asia's middle class

No matter how you segment and target the middle class, however, the future seems to be rosy. For example, consider the projected income figures published by McKinsey for China. In an article titled "Meet the Chinese Consumer of 2020," McKinsey presents an economic profile of Chinese consumers at the end of this decade. They predict that income differences will persist, but will shift drastically. From 2010 to 2020, the share of "poor" urban households (defined as earning less than USD 6,000 annually) will decrease from 10 to 7 per cent, and the "value" segments (USD 6,000–15,999) will decrease from 82 to 36 per cent. In contrast, the share of the "mainstream" segment (USD 16,000–34,000) will increase from 6 per cent to 51 per cent, a projected compound annual growth rate of 26.6 per cent. Finally, the affluent segment (above USD 34,000) will grow as well, but less, from 2 to 6 per cent.

The report also predicts that it will be easier and more worthwhile to enter the hinterland. In 2010, in the 100 wealthiest cities, there were 85 per cent of mainstream consumers. In the next 300 wealthiest cities, there were only 10 per cent of mainstream consumers. By 2020, however, this number will increase to 30 per cent. Thus, the drastic city-by-city (or urban-rural) differences will disappear in the future, creating new markets for companies.

Even if these projections were too optimistic, the trend spells good news for many companies and make up a key argument for targeting the middle class (from lower to core to upper-middle). Companies will have a large segment of middle-class consumers that have enough disposable income and purchasing power in the coming years. As companies focus on these consumers in the future, they will be more profitable than ever.

08

STANDARDIZATION VERSUS LOCALIZATION
CAN YOU PURSUE A PAN-ASIAN STRATEGY?

Companies need to take local realities into account. But a more generalized approach is desirable

At a broad level, companies operating across Asian markets face a choice between a pan-Asian segmentation strategy, where all Asians are treated the same way, versus different strategies for individual markets. In short, should there be standardization across markets or localization?

Choosing between two extremes

It appears that the most logical way for marketers is to pursue a pan-Asian strategy. It makes things simple, straightforward, and efficient. Moreover, through a wide-angle lens, all Asians seem to share similar values and similar histories, and have similar economic development paths. Thus, their purchase desires and shopping behaviors should be treated equally. It would also seem that a pan-Asian strategy would provide focus; it would create economies of scale in manufacturing and save marketing costs.

However, if we sharpen our lens and look at the details, there also seems to be immense diversity across the different markets, and hence, diverse consumer preferences across the East Asia region. Many companies therefore feel that it is impossible to pursue a pan-Asian strategy or even regional strategies for, say, North Asia (e.g., Korea and Japan), China (including the People's Republic of China, Hong Kong, and Taiwan), the Indian subcontinent (India, Pakistan, and Sri Lanka) or Southeast Asia (from Indo-China to Malaysia and Indonesia).

What is more, standardization may hurt your business. We must be cautious to avoid the fallacy of believing "what works in Japan will also work in Korea," as my colleague and friend Professor Dae Ryun Chang of Yonsei University in Seoul, South Korea, pointed out. In some Asian countries, he argued, even the internal diversity is high— China, India, and Indonesia are like continents in terms of how many different ethnic groups, languages, and regional preferences each possesses. Indeed, China's beer market, the largest in the world, is so fragmented that the major breweries like Yanjing and Tsingtao have to use a multiregional brand strategy to appeal to each local market. Tsingtao, for example, has adapted its beer bottle for Chengdu consumers so that beer can easily be poured into small cups and shared over Sichuan food the way Chinese liquor is drunk. The message seems clear: there is no "one Asia" and there cannot be a pan-Asian strategy. What we need is localization.

Because of the presumed diversity of Asia's cultures, ethnicities, and languages, most companies run their business on a regional basis—India, China, Indonesia, and ASEAN markets, for example—and manage some of their brands on a country-by-country basis. This approach also appears to be "culturally sensitive."

"There is no Asian consumer"

At the Asia Business Summit that ACI co-organizes with the *Financial Times*, I have heard this point of view echoed many times. For example, at the 2012 summit, I had with me on stage Peter ter Kulve, Executive Vice President, Southeast Asia and Australasia for Unilever. When I asked him, "How do you define an Asian consumer? What actually is an Asian consumer?" he declared:

> *Anybody who defines a consumer as an "Asian consumer" probably has not been long enough in the region, because they don't exist. It is even impossible to create marketing programs for consumers in Southeast Asia. This is our management name. But there is not even such a thing as Indonesian consumers. There are Sumatran consumers, there are Javanese consumers, and there are consumers in Kalimantan, with their own culture, their own habits and their own value system.*

PepsiCo's Umran Beba, President of the company's Asia-Pacific operations, who also shared the stage with me, was less adamant and more cautious. After all, of PepsiCo's 22 global brands, 14

SCHMITT converses with the expert of the Region

are available in Asia. However, it is the regional brands that are becoming more successful and powerful in various markets.

One of PepsiCo's regional brands is Sting Energy Drink, which was created in Vietnam. "Today Sting is also in Pakistan and the Philippines and we are looking beyond these three markets to places where Sting can grow," she said. "We also have a very iconic potato chip brand, Smith's, in Australia, and Red Rock Deli, which was created in Australia and now, actually moving to other markets." So, at least some brands can move from one market to the next.

In the future, as Asian economies grow, and more and more people enter the middle class, global brands may further increase market share. "One thing that is very important is that consumers are becoming wealthier and, of course, the aspirational brands become very important," she says. "Brands that underline good quality and the great taste that consumers are looking for are the sort of things PepsiCo offers with this kind of aspirational branding."

But even global brands, like Pepsi or Frito-Lay, PepsiCo's potato chip brand, need to be localized in the actual marketing campaigns. "Our potato chips are really quite a Western kind of product, but you have to really make it very relevant," says Beba. "In China, we launched our cooling cucumber flavor potato chip because, in the beginning, the Lay's Potato Chip was not very relevant to Chinese consumers who have a 'heating' and 'cooling' concept about their food. Over time we've adopted this and created these flavors." Part of localization is also showing that you care about the local community. "There is a huge gap between the high end and the low end, and we have to make sure for our consumers' communities that we undertake the right citizenship activities," adds Beba. In the Philippines, PepsiCo has two projects that address the needs of the community. The first, Water Hope, is a collaboration between the company and local social entrepreneurs, most of them women, to build safe drinking water stations. The second project, called Litre of Light, uses an ingenious recycling concept, creating solar powered light bulbs from PET bottles filled with water and bleach.

The balanced view

Thus, the following recipe for success seems to be emerging. First, a diversified company needs a portfolio of brands in Asian markets, and the right mix of global and local brands. Moreover, global brands need to be localized

"I have 23 countries reporting to me"

in tactical marketing communications and implementations, and perhaps in the product and the core service to some degree. Yet, too much localization or customization has its pitfalls. First of all, some brands have clearly achieved global appeal and are desirable to consumers because of this global appeal. Furthermore, some brands that start out fairly local can be transferred to other markets. After all, a strategy that is too granular is not of much use because it requires immense resources, complexities, and costs to implement.

Rather than being overwhelmed and giving in to all the diversities that exist in the region, it is important to find the similarities and commonalities in consumer needs, preferences, and behaviors, and thus, find some structure in the market. Of course, Chinese consumers like watermelons and Thai consumers like lime juice, but that doesn't mean you can't sell Pepsi—and "pure" Pepsi for that matter, not watermelon or lime-flavored Pepsi—to these consumers. The ultimate segmentation scheme does not need to be "pan-Asian" but it should go across countries to examine potential similarities and communalities among Asian consumers. A Pan-Asian urban-rural scheme may be one such approach: to distinguish, for example, "world city consumers" from "secondary city consumers," or "consumers living on the fringes of cities" from "rural consumers." Another way to segment across Asia is based on lifestyle: "hedonic lifestyle seekers" versus "value-focused functionalists" or "image-conscious" versus "quality-driven." Yet another scheme may be based on attitudinal type distinguishing across Asia, for example, "the "detached" from "the strivers," "the satisfied," and "the accomplished," "In practice, based on consumer insight, such segmentations can also get far more detailed.

Methodologically and statistically, the first step is to generate such a generalized segmentation scheme based on similarities among Asian consumers, and then subsequently to determine how important and significant a particular segmentation scheme is in a particular country. After that, numerical country differences in individual segments (pan-Asian or country-specific) should be assessed as well. I favor such an empirical and statistical approach because it allows for both the similarities and differences among Asian consumers to emerge rather than to predicate them. This is the only valid way of segmenting the diverse Asian markets, and yet none of the research agencies and consulting firms I know use this approach.

The key question to ask is "Under what condition is a more general segmentation scheme likely to work?" First, such an approach is more likely to be successful for certain product categories than others. Products closely related to the basics of daily life such as food products, personal care products, and related services (food delivery and cleaning services) are probably not the right pick for such an approach. They are very local. A Chinese prefers different flavors more than an Indian or Korean consumer does. Some personal care and household items can be local as well. However, the more upscale these food or cosmetics products are, the more likely they can be marketed more globally and in a standardized fashion. Take luxury brands: they rightly use the same appeal all across Asia and across the world, because they are expected to lead consumer tastes and preferences. Technology products, financial products, and pharmaceuticals are likely to be in the same category as luxury products: they also have similar needs across markets.

Another factor to consider is the consumer. The most uniform desires and preferences can be found at the bottom and top end of the market. Relatively poor, first-time consumers will have less developed preferences than consumers at the core of the middle class. They are looking for good, cheap products, and the brand is a secondary consideration. And affluent Asian consumers have preferences that are similar to those of their counterparts in other parts of the world. They are international in their outlook, drawn to the same brands, and expect similar services. It is the middle class that requires a heavy dose of localization. They tend to be choosy. They want the right product for themselves. They remind me of the demanding passengers sitting in business class. People in economy class do not expect much; those in first class are very relaxed. But people in business class want it their way.

Finally, whether you can use a more general segmentation or need to be more detailed in your approach also depends on the size of a market (say, the size of a country). That is, preferences of consumers in smaller countries (Vietnamese or Singaporeans) are likely to be more uniform than those of Chinese, Indian, and Indonesian consumers. In large countries, segmentation and then localization by region may be one approach. Another way is to perform lifestyle segmentation within the country.

For example, with 28 states and 22 official languages and a strong urban-rural gap, India is extremely diverse, and must be segmented on its own. Indonesia, too, is large and diverse; McKinsey presented an attitudinal segmentation of Indonesia with seven consumer segments: "pragmatic strivers," "middle-aged conservatives," "middle-aged optimists," the "frugal middle class," "virtuous well-offs," "well-off modern adults," and "emerging well-off youths." An attitudinal, lifestyle, or marketing-related segmentation may also be done for large cities when these cities are key markets in a country. In 1997, when the Chinese consumer revolution was getting into full swing, I conducted a segmentation study in two of the key commercial cities: Beijing and Shanghai. The segmentation scheme distinguished four distinct segments: "market rejecters," "marketing affected," "brand explorers," and "traditional functionalists."

It's all about the right cut

Segmentation strategy, after all, is about cutting the market the right way. That cut should neither be too broad nor too narrow. Most importantly, it should be based on consumer insight applied to meaningful product and brand-related similarities and differences among Asian consumers. Such insight can help you in your choice on whether to use a more standardized or more localized approach.

09

CORPORATE IMAGE
BRANDS, BRANDS, BRANDS

A foreign image still works.
However, Asian brand identities
and experiences are on the rise

Asians have caught a new disease. An infectious and contagious one. One that cannot be cured. And thus far, no vaccine, not even a recession, has been effective. Branditis.

The disease for brands started three decades ago in Japan. It then spread to the new growth economies of Hong Kong, Singapore, Taiwan, and South Korea. (The Supreme Leader of North Korea had successfully taken protective measures.) When it broke out in mainland China, it was considered a serious epidemic. Now it is affecting consumers all over Asia. Symptoms of branditis include a compulsion for the latest brands, spending sleepless nights worrying about not getting the right ones, and experiencing serious depression when the brand is not available.

Among Asian women, branditis is most prevalent for luxury apparel and handbag brands. For men, it has had its highest incidence rate for cars, smartphones, and other consumer electronics. Both sexes are about equally affected by fast-moving consumer goods. Branditis has also been observed for services: some consumers have experienced a catatonic depression when they could not purchase a room in a particular hotel, book a certain airline, or buy a certain property.

Asian's obsession with brands

Asian consumers' obsessive compulsion with brands had its origin in a desire for quality, consistency, and value. Asians equate brands, and the premium prices that they command, with high quality. But owning a brand is also about status and prestige. In fact, the latter two intangibles are frequently the primary reason for purchasing a certain brand. For consumers who have just entered the middle class, acquiring a brand is a signal for having superior knowledge as a consumer, which reflects a status. For the core middle class, buying brands is a way to display a newly acquired position in society. For upper middle-class consumers, it is about showing off one's disposable income. Finally, for the affluent, consuming brands means being part of brand communities of people who think alike: they have the same taste, style, or lifestyle. In sum, for consumers at all levels, owning a brand reflects societal status and prestige.

But what type of brands do Asian consumers prefer?

Give me a global brand …

Research has revealed time and again that Asians prefer foreign, global brands over local brands, and are willing to pay a premium price for it. Foreign typically means Western. The desirable country of origin of the Western brand depends on the product category. For example, Asian consumers prefer fashion products from France or Italy, and cars from Germany. In consumer packaged goods, the brands of three Western companies—Unilever, Procter & Gamble, and Nestle–dominate in most markets, according to Kantar's Brand Footprint ranking. Western brands seem to have something that most Asian brands don't have: they have a long history; they have quality and style; and they are known globally.

Most importantly, they are the original. According to Paul Temporal, author of the book *Branding in Asia*, Asian companies have not placed brand building high on their priority list. Instead, for many

Apple, designed in California

decades there has been a copying and knock-off mentality among Asian firms. This mentality has been encouraged by weak intellectual property laws. Many Asian companies are good at copying the look, feel, and quality of a brand. From a purely product quality point of view, I hear that the Berkin and Kelly bags you can get in Itaewon in Seoul, South Korea, tend to be close in quality to the originals. Many new Asian brands (such as Singapore's TWG brand of teas and tea houses) also seem to imitate the positioning of similar Western brands (for example, the French top-end tea brand Marriage) and use Western brand naming and imagery (TWG calls itself the "grands crus prestige" of teas). They try to cover up their Asian origins. But a knowledgeable Asian consumer will be able to tell and will care.

In branding, Western firms have an advantage. A pure engineering and "follower" mentality cannot produce a great brand. Branding is about design, image, creativity, and innovation. To keep their competitive edge, Western firms should continue their successful global positioning, anchored in a country market of origin. It is also critical for Western brands to continue to deliver innovative products and not to underestimate Asians by introducing second- or third-generation products. Innovative products should even be launched first in Asia. Most importantly, you must show success beyond Asia. Asian consumers know what's going on elsewhere in the world;

they cannot be fooled into believing that a brand is a "famous global brand" when it is not—or no longer.

How about an Asian identity?

While Western brands still carry a cachet, increasingly prominent brands from Asia are becoming attractive to Asian consumers as well. For example, it is no longer unusual for a consumer from Thailand or Malaysia to opt for a Japanese brand for a car or air-conditioner, a Korean brand for a smartphone, and a Taiwanese brand for a computer. This is likely to be the case for two reasons. First, the

Coming to a town near you

brands (say, Toyota or Mitsubishi from Japan, Samsung from Korea, or Acer from Taiwan) are associated with countries that are seen as more advanced in their development than one's own country. Second, they are less seen as Asian than as global trademarks. Also, as a country develops, Asians proudly buy, wear, and display the successful brands from this country. Hence, it is hard to find a Korean with a non-Korean smartphone or flat screen television brand.

Knowledgeable consumers are also increasingly aware that many Western brands are made in Asia. So, how Western then is the brand really, especially as some Western companies have moved not only their manufacturing to Asia, but also their design and innovation teams?

Some experts feel that Asian consumers may therefore tire of Western trademarks and embrace their own cultures as the continent gains more influence in the world. Julien Cayla, a professor at Nanyang Technological University and a research fellow at ACI, has spoken with advertising executives and brand managers in Asia, and observed that some of them are now trying to create transnational Asian brands, with a perception of Asia as urban, modern, and multicultural. Brands such as Singapore's Tiger Beer, Hong Kong's Giordano, and Zuji, an online travel portal, have used such imagery in advertising. A major Korean airline calls itself "Asiana." Since 2006 DBS, a Singapore bank, has run a corporate campaign ("Living, Breathing Asia") in order to build the image of an Asian bank that understands the needs of Asians. As Cayla writes in a paper titled "Asian Brands and the Shaping of a Transnational Imagined Community" (co-authored with Giana Eckhardt), these brands seem to realize the dream of Singaporean singer Dick Lee, who in 1991 expressed the idea of a transfigured Asian identity in his song "Orientalism":

> I think it's time to show / That all of us are no
> Caricatures or stereotypes / No token yellows!
> We simply have to be / Assertive, make them see
> This is the new Asian / Ready for the twenty-first century.

It remains to be seen how widespread this approach will be in the future and how broadly Asian consumers will accept it. If it is successful, then Western brands that carry an Asian identity need to launched. In the apparel business, both at the mass-market and high-end level, this is happening already. In 2010, U.S. jeans maker Levi Strauss launched its Denizen denim brand first in Asia and only a year later in the United States. The brand is currently available in China, India, Pakistan, and Singapore. (Interestingly, the brand likes to be known as "dENiZEN"—note the "ZEN" in the name.) Also in 2010, Hermes, the French luxury brand, launched Shang Xia—clothing, accessories, and home décor items (such as furniture pieces, jewelry, and table settings) in Shanghai. It has a store in Shanghai and Beijing, and a Paris store is planned for late 2013. However the brand has thus far not been particularly successful.

I want to experience it ...

Some Asian consumers, especially younger Asians, want more than a name, trademark or logo; they are looking for lifestyle: Young women like products that are fashionable and cute (the Japanese call it "kawaii"); men want brands that are cool and techno-hip. They want to touch, feel, imagine, interact with, and relate to a brand—in short, they want a brand experience.

To capitalize on this trend, firms operating in the region need to move from features-and-benefits marketing to what I call "experiential marketing." Experiential marketers ask how a brand fits into consumers' lifestyles.

The kawaii experience

They create brand experiences associated with style, feelings, creativity, and the like. For example:

- **SENSE experiences appeal to the senses through sight, sound, touch, taste, and smell; they are aesthetically appealing and exciting (for example, many brands in fashion, media, and entertainment).**

- **FEEL experiences appeal to customers' feelings and emotions, and present emotional brand symbols (such as Hello Kitty).**

- **THINK experiences appeal to the intellect and creative imagination. They are often found in corporate advertising campaigns (e.g., HSBC's prominent campaigns in the region).**

- **ACT** experiences enrich customers' lives by targeting actions as well interactions (as many social media brands do).

- **RELATE** experiences expand beyond individuals' personal feelings using appeals to family, group relations, even the nation, which is important for the Asian collectivist mindset. (Tata Enterprises was very successful in marketing its cars by appealing to Indian pride.)

Starbucks is a experiential brand that has revolutionized the Asian coffee market and encouraged numerous local startup copycats. The Starbucks brand is holistic: it creates a multisensory experience; it also provides a good feeling, gets consumers to think through new coffee offers, encourages actions and interactions at its stores, and fosters relations.

Coffee in Xin Tian Di

Experiential marketing on a pan-Asian scale raises a range of key strategic questions: Do consumers in different Asian countries or cultures expect and appreciate the same type of experience? Do consumers in one market prefer FEEL, and in a second market THINK, and in a third RELATE? Are certain Asian consumer segments more attuned to aesthetics in SENSE, while others love excitement. Do some like nationalistic RELATE appeals but others global appeals?

... but it also needs to work

Whereas some Asian consumers, and especially, the young generation, seem to be attracted to brand experiences, for others an experiential appeal may not be their primary concern. They are still focused on functionality instead, and on the performance and quality of a brand. For them, the brand needs to have the right features and benefits, and work well.

I learned this lesson in a research project that I conducted with my colleague Kamel Jedidi at Columbia Business School in New York and Lia Zarantonelli at IESEG School of Management in Paris. We analyzed a dataset of 256 TV commercials provided by a multinational fast-moving consumer goods firm. The data included 23 developed and emerging markets (including the Asian markets of China, India, Indonesia, Pakistan, the Philippines, Thailand, and Vietnam). We considered two types of communications: functional communications, which emphasize the features and benefits of a product, and experiential communications, which evoke sensations, feelings, and imaginations. We found that whereas in developed markets the experiential route mostly drove communication persuasion, the functional route was still a relatively more important driver in emerging markets.

To appeal to Asian consumers' brand consciousness, the right approach is critical. For some consumers, the brand should be international; for others, brands need to have a local appeal. For some, it is still about functionality; but others want an all-out experience. As a result, depending on the insights that you have gained about your target consumers, the best strategy may be a global or localized, and a functional or experiential, approach.

10

STRATEGY TOOL 1
THE ASIA
STRATEGY MAP™

How to plot a long-term roadmap for your business

ASIA STRATEGY MAP

	BASIC	INTERMEDIATE	ADVANCED
1. What do you know about Asian Markets?	Assess Asian market basics	Assess industry specific market information	Evaluate future market potential and limitations
2. Where is the product-market fit?	Is there a basic product-market fix?	Evaluate new product potential in Asian markets	Assess continuous innovation potential
3. What do you know about your Asian customers?	Determine basic needs of Asian customers	Understand emotional needs of Asian customers	Uncover latent and unarticulated needs
4. How can you make money?	Create business model outline	Assess sustainability of your business model in Asia	Evaluate future risks
5. What is required from the business to work in Asia?	Determine basic organizational requirements	Assess specific organizational structures and processes	Assess future organizational potential to succeed in Asia

To succeed and thrive in Asia, you need a long-term strategic focus. You need to decide whether you should pursue a pan-Asian strategy or take a local approach; whether you should focus at the bottom, middle, or top of the pyramid; and whether your brand image should be global or Asian. To accomplish your strategic tasks, you need the right maps and tools to get your analyses done. I will therefore provide you with a portfolio of strategic and analytical maps and tools, which we have used at ACI in Singapore in client projects.

This portfolio of tools is based, in part, on studies conducted by researchers associated with ACI and consulting work with clients. They are practical tools for decision makers, similar to other strategic tools (such as the Growth-Share Matrix, The Balanced Score Card, or the Blue Ocean Strategy Canvas). They help you as a manager to gain clarity and reach decisions on the key issues that you are facing in Asian markets – today and in the future.

Here is my first tool for you: the Asia Strategy Map™. It helps you to outline a competitive long-term strategy for Asian markets. It will address the above questions—and more. It will also help you with specific decision issues, for example, which products to launch in which Asian markets, which customer targets to focus on, and which business model to use.

The Asia Strategy Map™ consists of answering questions that fall into five broad strategy categories. Each question can be subdivided into several more specific questions. To address the issues in each of the five categories, I recommend a three-step procedure.

As a first step, list what you know with certainty, based on general data, information, management knowledge, and expertise. Call this the "basic box."

Second, identify and formulate a series of specific questions—for example, three to five questions that relate to your industry, your products or services, and your customers. These questions are vital, in fact, more vital than the information in the basic box. Most likely, you already have some information, or at least a good guess, for providing answers to these questions. Call this the "intermediate box."

As part of the third step, you identify advanced questions that you may not be able to answer right away. These questions may require additional data collection, advanced market research, and sophisticated forecasts. At this point, you may leave the answer sheet blank. Just be aware of these questions and collect the information as it comes in, so that you can improve your strategy map. Call this box "the advanced box."

Strategy category 1:
What do you know about Asian markets?

You need some basic information about Asian markets. I shared with you some of this type of information at the beginning of this book—about predicted economic growth, the rise of the middle class, consumption, and disposable incomes for the region. You also need country-by-country data and current and future data on specific demographics (men/women, age, and income). Put this information in your basic box and use it to determine whether a specific Asian market is worth your attention, and whether it constitutes an opportunity.

Then you move on to the intermediate box to identify questions and information needs that relate specifically to your industry and your business. It is a skill to ask the right questions. You are no longer just considering a potential opportunity; you will be using the information in the intermediate box for a preliminary go/no go decision for your business. Therefore, you need to ask the right questions to get the right answers.

Finally, in the advanced box, you are asking for further details that will help you in the actual market entry. What will be your point of entry? How can you expect to grow your business in this market? What are the limitations and challenges? Here you may need to commission new information and update this information from time to time.

Strategy category 2:
Where is the product-market fit?

To be successful in any business, you need to check whether there is a product-market fit, or more precisely, how such a fit may be achieved and further enhanced. Do you already have a "hit" product, or are you about to create a new product that will resonate with a target market? Which target market? Who are your potential customers?

In the basic box, you record the basic product-market fit. If there is such a fit, there's a go. You will most likely succeed to some degree with your products or services. But can you extract its fullest potential? To see how product-market fit could be further improved, you ask additional questions and put these questions, together with your answers, into the intermediate box. For example, what additional features or experiences will customers in this market desire? What new products will they be interested in? How could you get your customers to pay a higher price or increase volume? Finally, in the advanced box, you list complex or long-term questions that you may only be able to resolve after you have gained experience in the identified market(s).

Strategy category 3:
What do you know about your Asian customers?

Success in consumer markets requires a customer-centric strategy. Without understanding your customers in depth, you won't be able to address their needs, satisfy their desires and expectations, and make them happy. They may buy once (and worse, on impulse); but they won't return as customers.

Thus, you need to find out how well you understand your customers and what you know about them. In the basic box you list key facts that you know about your current or potential customers. This tells you what you need to do to deliver basic customer satisfaction— that is, fulfilling, but not necessarily, exceeding, their expectations. This also provides a basic check on whether your organization is customer-centric or not.

In the intermediate box, you list critical questions that may help you in providing a higher level of customer satisfaction and gaining a competitive advantage. For example, in your questions, you may move beyond functional expectations into the realms of feelings and emotions, and unspoken needs. What do you know about those emotional and perhaps unarticulated needs? Finally, in the advanced box, you may list questions that help you address future needs and desires, for example, as a market matures. Category 3 as a whole, and the advanced box in particular, require market research. Or you may use benchmark data and your intuition.

Strategy category 4:
How can you make money?

This strategy category concerns your business model. Let's say you have identified an attractive potential market. You have the right product for it, and you are customer-centric. How are you going to make money?

You sketch the broad outlines of your business model in the basic box. You ask additional questions about the details and sustainability of your business model in the intermediate box, and you list the answers. In the advanced box you list "what if" questions. What if the technology changes? What if a powerful player enters the market or upgrades its capabilities? What if the profile of customers changes radically?

Strategy category 5:
What is required from the business to work in Asia?

Finally, you need to determine what internal structures and processes the business needs to implement in order to be successful. In the basic box, you assess the business basics and the core competencies required. In the intermediate and advanced boxes you determine the necessary intermediate and advanced structures and processes for management, finance and accounting, HR, operations, sales, and marketing? Success is often found in the details. Be as specific as possible in answering these organizational and implementation questions.

A roadmap for your business

You are done with the Asia Strategy Map™. You now have a

customer-focused strategy and a roadmap for your business. You have sketched a long-term strategic perspective on Asia that provides you with guidance and structure on how to make critical decisions as they arise.

Note that the Asia Strategy Map™ helps you to answer the "big questions." Answers within strategy categories 1–3, in particular, will help you with the decision on whether or not you can pursue a pan-Asian strategy, or whether you need to engage local market-by-market strategies, and which level of the market (bottom, middle, top) your business should address. Answers in strategy categories 2 and 3 also tell you what image (local or international) your customers will prefer. In addition, the Asia Strategy Map™ points to specific changes required in your product and approach toward customers, your business model, and organization as a whole.

One more note. I advise that you also perform a competitive analysis along the way. How good is your competitors' product-market fit? Are your products better or cheaper than those of your competitors, or do you have a stronger brand? How much do your competitors know about customers? What's their business model? Organizationally, what are their core competencies? If you perform the analyses suggested in this chapter thoroughly, you are well on your way to plotting a viable competitive strategy for Asian markets for the long haul.

11

STRATEGY TOOL 2
THE CONCEPT EXPLORATION METHOD™

How to discover new market opportunities

A culture affects how we view the world—for example, what and whom we consider beautiful, healthy, or clean. Ask yourself:

- *What is beauty? What are the features and characteristics of a beautiful woman, and a beautiful man? What makes a landscape beautiful?*

- *What is healthy? What is fitness? What is healthy food? What's a fit body? What does it mean that somebody lives a healthy—or "fitness"—lifestyle?*

- *What is cleanliness? What do we mean when we say that a kitchen top, a bathroom, a piece of clothing is "clean"? What exactly is "cleanliness"?*

People in different cultures differ drastically in what and whom they consider to be beautiful, healthy, or clean. Thus, when you run a business in the beauty or health industry or sell cleaning products, you need a method to explore what these concepts mean to your customers, especially in the culturally diverse Asian region. To accomplish this task, I am offering you here the Concept Exploration Method™.

Cultures and concepts

For individuals in some cultures, beauty is looks. And you are born with it: you either have it or you don't. For others, beauty is like a personality trait; you become more beautiful as you grow and increase your confidence. Some cultures consider delicate features and a small nose beautiful. For others, it is big breasts and tight buttocks. Likewise, for individuals in some cultures, health and fitness is how you look. For others, health and fitness can only be determined through a medical examination. And some equate cleanliness with hygiene whereas others view it largely as orderliness.

CONCEPT EXPLORATION METHOD™

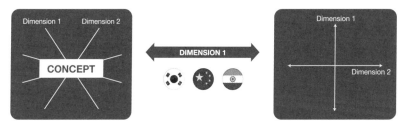

For illustration only

Culture is, in part, reflected in art. In Chinese art, beauty is seen as graciousness and humbleness. In the arts of Indo-China and the Indian subcontinent, beauty is more outward: luscious figures swinging their bodies. For a Chinese, a person's health or fitness as well as healthy food and a healthy lifestyle may be assessed based on Chinese philosophy, medicine, and cultural traditions. Tai chi differs greatly from weightlifting. Similarly, the concept of cleanliness is closely intertwined with cultural concepts of the body, personal space, and the environment in which a person lives.

There are many other daily-life, consumption-related concepts that are cultural in nature. What is "a vacation"? Is it simply the absence of work? Is it engaging in certain activities (like lying on the beach or hiking in the mountains)? Or what is travel? Is it going from one place to another or exploring one place in depth? What moods and thoughts come to your mind when you think of your last vacation or travel? Travel agents, airlines, hotels and resorts, and any employer need to understand what its customers and employees mean by vacation, and by travel.

Or take luxury. What do we mean by luxury? Are luxury goods merely expensive? Or do they need to be handcrafted so that we can feel the maker or the artist behind the product? Or are they simply a logo or trademark put on a product?

In any business, you need to understand such concepts and how consumers perceive the very essence of your business. Here is a method that explores the essential concept of a business in order to discover new business opportunities. At ACI, we have used the Concept Exploration Method with companies in various businesses to help them understand how their customers view the business, its products, and brands.

The Concept Exploration Method™ consists of three steps.

Step 1: Concept deconstruction

The term "deconstruction," borrowed from the field of literary criticism, has been defined as "a project of critical thought whose task is to locate and 'take apart' those concepts which serve as the axioms or rules," as "a systematic un-doing of understanding," and, more simply as "cracking nutshells." In a very Asian philosophical way, Jacques Derrida, a French philosopher and literary critic, who was a prominent figure in this field, wrote that "there is nothing outside the text" *(il n'y a pas de hors-texte)*, meaning that the "context" is an integral part of the text. In other words, concepts of beauty, health and cleanliness, travel and luxury are closely intertwined with a culture; they have no context-independent, transcendent, or essentialist meaning.

Accordingly, the first step of the Concept Exploration Method™ uses cultural analysis to deconstruct and contextualize a concept by showing how it is tied to other cultural concepts, and creates its meaning from it. For example, the concept of health in Chinese culture is closely tied to Chinese medicine (the concept of yin and yang foods, of warm and cold) and Chinese philosophy (e.g., the concepts of balance and moderation), as well as cultural rituals and practices (breathing, relaxation, and movement techniques such as qi gong, tai chi, and meditation). Thus, when we present a product as "healthy" to a Chinese consumer who is embedded in such belief systems, we need to be aware of the entire meaning structure that is associated with it.

Concept deconstruction, performed to identify the deep meaning of a concept usually results in around ten workable dimensions— or "facets of meaning." They may emerge from the analysis of cultural texts (such as beauty, fitness or travel magazines; ads for cleaning or luxury products; art objects, consumer products and other artifacts; pop culture or consumer rituals) and may be supplemented or validated based on textual and visual analysis of online conversations, expert interviews, IdeaBlast™.

Step 2: Cultural mapping

Next, consumer groups from different cultures (e.g., Chinese, Indians, Indonesians), countries (China, Korea, Japan), or consumer segments (e.g., geographical segments of northern versus southern Chinese, or Chinese from first- versus second-tier cities; or age segments of teenagers, young adults, mid-life, and senior citizens; or lifestyle segments such as "the young and fun," "the active types," and "the relaxed types") are represented on each concept dimension. This is often done based on empirical analysis. In his theory of deconstruction, Derrida used the term "binary opposition" (i.e., terms that are opposite in their meanings). As a result, the concept dimensions are frequently bipolar in nature.

For example, the concept of beauty may be deconstructed along the bipolar dimensions of "inner versus outer beauty" and the typical perceptions of cultures, countries, or consumer segments may be represented in terms of where they rank on the scale. Similarly, the bipolar dimension of "inborn/cannot be changed versus can be changed by technology" may represent traditionally minded Indians on one end and plastic-surgery approving Koreans at the other end. Finally, a dimension of "individual versus social" (meaning a personality concept of beauty based on personal self-esteem versus one that includes the role in society of a person that may make her/him more or less beautiful) may plot relatively individualistic Hong Kong consumers on one end, and traditional Indonesian consumers at the other end.

Cultural mapping also helps us to examine whether one standard of beauty (a pan-Asian concept, or perhaps a global concept of beauty) may be emerging. If there is sufficient evidence for such a concept in consumers' minds, then product and communications may be marketed similarly and with a global appeal. And a woman, or man, representing this concept may be chosen as a representative model and brand allegory.

Step 3: New concept application
Insights from deconstructing a concept and its cultural mapping will allow the company and its management to create a new concept and apply it as part of a new product launch, brand repositioning, or other new initiatives.

Assume that the deconstruction and cultural mapping of the concept of luxury resulted in a new concept of "barely branded, intimate luxury," which has appeal to a significant segment of Asian consumers in key metropolitan world cities such as Shanghai, Hong Kong, or Bangkok. This may point to a line of minimally branded, no big-logo luxury goods, or a retail chain with select merchandise of small brands from around the world, or a subtle social media campaign and web presence. Similarly, the concept of a "vacation at home" may point to new, perhaps luxurious offers of home delivery during such a "vacation" period and a vacation package of dining, leisure, and cultural offers during the vacation in one's home town.

Discovering new market opportunities
The Concept Exploration Method™ is a perfect method for discovering new opportunities in Asian markets. By deconstructing

an existing concept, enriching and mapping it culturally, and then applying the new concept, the method produces innovative business solutions that can launch new concepts in a marketplace. These concepts have the potential of revamping an industry. It is therefore certainly worthwhile to leave one's business-as-usual attitude behind to explore more significant, potentially market-changing options. The culturally diverse Asian markets are a perfect place for such an disruptive initiative.

12

STRATEGY TOOL 3
THE ASIAN LIFESTYLE TOOL™

How to design customized products and services

THE ASIAN LIFESTYLE TOOL™

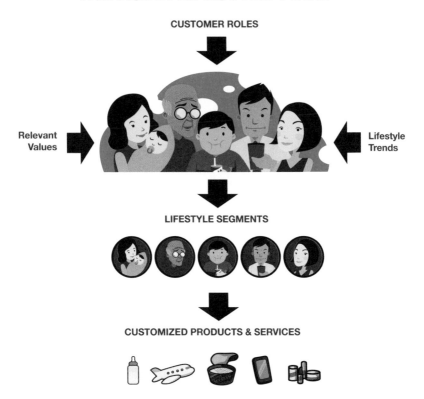

CUSTOMER ROLES

Relevant Values

Lifestyle Trends

LIFESTYLE SEGMENTS

CUSTOMIZED PRODUCTS & SERVICES

To help companies launch better lifestyle-focused products and services for Asian customers, I have developed the Asian Lifestyle Tool™. Many businesses these days are impacted by consumer lifestyles. For example, next time you check into a business hotel in Asia (such as an Asia based chain like the Shangri-La, Mandarin-Oriental, or Taj Hotel, or an international chain like the Ritz-Carlton, Hyatt, or Hilton), I'd like you to reflect for a moment about the type of business traveler you are. Are you the type that loves attentive service from check-in to check-out? Or the type that loves to be acknowledged and recognized? Or are you the excited type, always on the lookout for something new to do? Or perhaps you are the relaxed type who wants to be left alone and just enjoy your stay in peace?

Having spent hundreds of nights in Asian hotels over the last 20 plus years myself, I can assure you this: in Asian hotels you are well taken care of. There is meticulous attention to details from the moment you enter the hotel, walk up to the front desk, and present your passport and credit card, to when you get to your room and begin to use the lavish facilities (the fitness clubs and spas, restaurant and business facilities, not to mention the club floors) to when you check out. Yet, I also feel they could do even better, in fact, much better, by considering the lifestyle of the traveler, and then, customizing the products and services for him or her.

I know which type of traveler I am. I am the efficient type. I value my time and don't want to waste it. Too much attentive service, and acknowledgments or recognition (such as "Welcome to hotel X, Mr. Schmitt! May I have your credit card, Mr. Schmitt? Thank you for your credit card. Sorry for keeping you waiting, Mr. Schmitt") don't do anything for me. They just waste my time. I am also not the "excited type;" I do look for new things, but not in a hotel. I would rather go out of the hotel, to a concert hall or art exhibition. My values and lifestyle are just different from some of the other guests, and I am still looking for the hotel that perfectly fits my lifestyle.

The Asian Lifestyle Tool™ identifies relevant broad-based values in life that impact consumer behavior, coupled with relevant lifestyle trends, that is, how customers want to live today. The tool also considers a customer's professional or private role (e.g., as a business traveler, as a doctor or a nurse, as a family man or woman). Based on all of this information, the tool categorizes you as one consumer type or another, and aligns products and services to you accordingly.

The Asian Lifestyle Tool™ includes five steps.

Step 1: Identify relevant values

Philosophers, psychologists, and sociologists have created

different schemes that present values or long-term personal needs and aspirations. You may know Maslow's hierarchy of needs, for example, with food and shelter as lower-order needs at the bottom, and needs for belonging, self-esteem, and self-actualization as higher-order needs at the top. Another scheme, specifically focused on values, is the so-called Value Survey by Milton Rokeach, a social psychologist. He distinguished 18 terminal values ("end states"): true friendship, mature love, self-respect, happiness, inner harmony, equality, freedom, pleasure, social recognition, wisdom, salvation, family security, national security, a sense of accomplishment, a world of beauty, a world at peace, a comfortable life, and an exciting life.

Let's apply Rokeach's model to the hotel situation discussed earlier. Clearly not all values are relevant. But some are. My concern for efficiency may originate from a general value of a sense of accomplishment. Other hotel guests may be more concerned about being socially recognized, or they may desire inner harmony, or a comfortable life, or an exciting life. These broad-based guiding principles seem to reflect themselves in the behavior of business hotel guests. In other words, selecting relevant values from Rokeach's value survey or other value schemes, and then applying them to a particular product or service, can be the starting point of a lifestyle analysis. But—wait, there is more. We must also consider current lifestyle trends that affect customers.

Step 2: Apply lifestyle trends

Consumer behavior is not only the result of values; equally important and influential are current lifestyle trends. So, we must take a look in the box of trend experts and see which trends may apply in a particular business. Here are three trends that may be relevant for hotels.

First, wellness. Nowadays, we all seem to feel that we need to be good to ourselves from time to time and get a massage, or do yoga, or light up a candle and soak in a bath with sea salt, and the like. This is a huge trend. The wellness business nowadays occupies a whole hall at *Maison et Objet*, the home décor tradeshow in Paris, and the must-go-to event for this industry. Clearly it is something to consider. And it explains the success of hotels and resorts that are banking on this trend (such as the Banyan Tree, with its Asian spa concept).

Second, time. People feel that their lives are busier than ever. (That's, in part, why they need to relax and focus on their wellness needs.) But time pressure also leads to other phenomena: not wasting time, appreciating time, sometimes taking time to recoup.

Third, technology. We are all surrounded by technology and can't escape it. Especially in Asia, people are on the constant lookout for the latest gadget. We believe that we need to be connected with colleagues, friends, and family all the time.

These trends, like values, create an influence behavior.

Step 3: Examine the customer's role

In addition to values and lifestyle trends, we need to consider the role of the customer. In the hotel example above, we assumed that our customer is a business traveler. While on business, a person is likely to behave differently than when they are on holiday—irrespective of their values and lifestyle trends. When traveling on business, there are meetings and tight schedules. You may be traveling with your team, or you may need to be in constant contact with your team. You are held accountable: you are supposed to produce results. And so on. That's the life of a business person and this will affect how he or she travel.

Step 4: Create lifestyle segments

Based on the identified relevant values, lifestyle trends, and role requirements, we can develop distinct lifestyle segments. Ideally, this is done empirically and quantitatively. That is, we measure the components of values, lifestyles, and roles, and then using statistical techniques, determine the number and type of customer lifestyle segments. Using the hotel example, they may be the "efficient traveler" (me), the "high-touch service traveler" (perhaps you), and other segments.

Step 5: Design customized products and services

Finally, we design relevant products and services for each lifestyle segment. We customize these offers for each segment. We no longer treat customers simply based on the price they pay and the room category we allocate to them, but as true individuals, especially our loyal customers. In sum, the idea is to provide them with products and services that resonate with their lifestyles.

I have illustrated the Asian Lifestyle Tool with an example from the hospitality business. I could have used soft drinks. If you are a diversified soft drinks, water, and juice company such as PepsiCo or the Coca-Cola Company, you need to do just the same. Your product development, positioning, and communications should be driven by lifestyle analysis. The same is true for technology products because they are increasingly becoming lifestyle products. In fact, almost any consumer market in Asia is increasingly a lifestyle market. Therefore, the Asian Lifestyle Tool is essential for capitalizing on this development.

13

STRATEGY TOOL 4
THE BRAND EXPERIENCE WHEEL™

How to transform a functional brand into an experience

THE BRAND EXPERIENCE WHEEL™

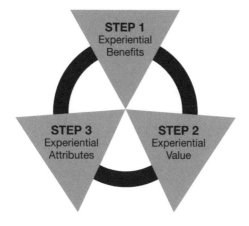

Many businesses in Asia are managed from an engineering perspective, resulting in an analytical approach. As a result, the products and brands may be of good quality but they provide mostly functional benefits. What is being neglected is the brand experience.

Since I wrote my books *Experiential Marketing* and *Customer Experience Management* I have advised several Asian firms on experience marketing and branding. Together with Japanese communications firm ADK, I have worked with Japanese clients to improve the brand experience. I have helped Korean skincare and cosmetics firm Amore Pacific in creating experiences for their various brands including Laneige, a successful brand sold all across Asia. I have written a case study on how Samsung Electronics has created an experiential digital camera. I have also done work on experiential marketing in Taiwan and Singapore.

Over the years, as part of this consulting for companies in Asia, I have developed and used various tools that turn functional marketing into experiential marketing. I am presenting here the Brand Experience Wheel™, a simple tool which we are also using in client work at ACI.

The Brand Experience Wheel™ helps you in transforming a product or brand from a functional into an experiential one. The Wheel achieves this transformation by focusing on experiential benefits, experiential value, and, finally, experiential attributes.

Experiential benefits

The starting point is an understanding of the nature of the brand. What benefits do the brand and its products currently provide to Asian customers? Out of the current benefits that the brand provides, management, perhaps jointly with a consultant, should brainstorm about potential experiential benefits that Asian customers may value and desire.

As discussed in the prior chapter on brand strategy, experiential benefits typically come in five forms: sensory, emotional, intellectual, behavioral, and relational benefits. Sensory benefits appeal to the senses. Emotional benefits are of a hedonic type—that is, positive feelings associated with a brand. Intellectual benefits appeal to customers' thoughts and imaginations. Behavioral benefits help customers to experience value-creating actions and interactions, and lifestyles. Finally, relational benefits include appeals to family and group relations.

Experiential value

This value is based on the experiential benefits. Experiential value can be measured and captured financially by assessing the price premium that may be charged because of the increased experiential utility. Many products these days are functionally equivalent but they may differ drastically in price. The luxury business is a great example. Asian consumers are willing to pay premium prices for luxury labels that are often hard to justify rationally. But what luxury products and the associated brands provide are positive feelings and experiential value. Such an intangible experience can be worth a lot of money.

Experiential attributes

Experiential attributes must be carefully designed after considering potential benefits and value. The experiential attributes are in fact providing the benefits that will result in value for the customer, and in turn, the company. They may be product characteristics or design elements that are part of the product. Many consumer electronics products these days are packed with experiential design features. As a result, Samsung has widely surpassed Sony in design and aesthetics, and as a result, in brand value.

In sum, the Brand Experience Wheel™ consists of three interrelated components – experiential benefits, experiential value, and experiential attributes – which need to be carefully planned to create a desirable product and brand experience. As we saw earlier in this book, Asian customers are crazy about brands. To be sure, a great brand delivers functionality and excellent quality. But what ultimately distinguishes one brand from another is the brand experience.

14

STRATEGY TOOL 5
ONLINE-OFFLINE MIX METRICS™

How to invest in an effective omni-channel strategy

ONLINE-OFFLINE MIX METRICS™

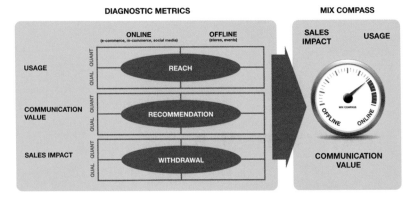

DIAGNOSTIC METRICS

MIX COMPASS

One of the key strategic concerns for companies in Asia today is designing a viable omni-channel strategy, and, in particular, the right mix of online and offline presence and media. For traditional retailers, this issue entails decisions such as, "Should we open new stores in a particular market or strengthen our online presence?", "What merchandise should we offer in the stores and online?", or "How should we price products in stores and online?" Conversely, an online seller may wonder whether or not to launch physical stores. Moreover, any company must ask itself to what degree it should invest resources into social media rather than into offline events or public relations activities.

In addition, there are broader strategic concerns about the role of online and offline channels and the online and offline experience. For example, as e-commerce, m-commerce, and social media are growing, how can companies best derive value from such channels and create the right experience for online shoppers and consumers? Or, as customers are increasingly "show-rooming" in stores, that is, exploring merchandise in stores but buying online because they get a better price or because it is more convenient, what is the role of stores in the future and how should they be designed, and be integrated with online channels, to create value for customers?

The Online-Offline Mix Metrics™ (or, in short, O2M2) tool provides a quantitative and qualitative measurement and strategy approach to these questions. In the O2M2 tool, "online" refers to e-commerce, m-commerce, and social media (e.g., Facebook, blogs, Twitter); "offline" refers to events and public relations as well as traditional advertising or call centers. O2M2 focuses on consumer usage patterns of relevant online and offline channels, their respective communication value, and sales impact by computing and delivering diagnostics about the nature of the consumer-channel relationship.

Diagnostic metrics

To determine usage, quantitative measures and qualitative assessments of "reach" are employed. They may be derived from company data or require additional market research. Reach refers to the total number of consumers that have used pertinent online and offline channels of the company within a specified time frame (say, during the last one to three months) and their assessment of the quality and experience with these channels. To determine communication value, a quantitative measure and qualitative assessment of "recommendations" are used. The quantitative measure is similar to the so-called "net promoter score," though adapted to the digital environment and Asian context; the qualitative assessment gauges the quality of recommendations to friends, colleagues, customers, and communities. Finally, for sales impact, the quantitative and qualitative assessments address "withdrawal"— that is, consumers' reactions if a channel were withdrawn from them or no longer available. Withdrawal may seem an extreme measure. However, this is intentional because O2M2 is supposed to help executives to reach the important strategic mix decision of online/ offline now and in the future rather than providing an overall status quo assessment of current sales.

Designing an omni-channel strategy

These diagnostic metrics are input to O2M2's Mix Compass.

Based on the measures and assessment for usage, communication value, and sales impact, the Mix Compass provides an overall recommendation regarding the degree and direction of online and offline channels—specifically, how much a company should employ online channels (relative to offline channels) now and in the future. For example, based on the illustration provided here, it would be recommended that the firm uses three quarters of online media (or 75 per cent) now. And based on future projections, it would be recommended to turn the entire business online in the future.

In sum, The Online-Offline Mix Metrics™ is a useful tool for making strategic and investment decisions concerning the right mix of online and offline channels. Like the other tools that are part of the strategy and analysis portfolio, this tool can help you address pressing business issues that you are facing in Asia now and in the future.

ASIAN M

In section 3, I will focus on Asian markets and businesses. I will present case studies and best practices from consumer electronics, apparel, food and beverage, and various services (including airlines, hotels, beauty and e-commerce).

Let's take off and immerse ourselv in the diversity of Asian markets.

ARKETS
ELECTRONICS
BUDGET AIRLINE
BEAUTY
INSTANT NOODLES
INSTANT NOODLES

Think of Asian markets, and two consumer-related industries and markets immediately come to mind: consumer electronics and apparel.

The electronics industry has recently shifted from a supplier mode towards developing powerful consumer brands, first in Japan, then in Taiwan and South Korea. By now the world knows not only consumer electronics brands such as Sony and Panasonic but also Acer and HTC as well as Samsung and LG.

The situation in apparel is different. Most of Asia is still a massive supplier of merchandise rather than a brand owner. The business has moved from country to country (from South Korea to China to Vietnam and Bangladesh, perhaps soon to Myanmar) to keep costs low. It seems timely to ask whether we will see the emergence of a global Asian fashion and lifestyle brand (excluding Japan) anytime soon.

Aside from consumer electronics and apparel, we will examine the food and beverages business. Foods and beverages are, arguably, the most local, culturally bound products. Nonetheless, foreign brands have been successful in Asia with their fast food chains and beverage brands for years. Now they are being challenged by fast-growing Asian firms.

The services sector is gaining in importance all over Asia. In fact, it is already huge in certain countries and further growing. For example, in 2012 it accounted for more than 70 per cent of nominal GDP in Singapore and for over 90 per cent in Hong Kong. It also contributed more than half of the GDP in other key Asian markets including South Korea, Taiwan, India, Thailand, and the Philippines.

Two services that fare prominently as world-class in Asia are airlines and hotels. Both are also known for a uniquely Asian style service concept. However, the airline and hotel industries in Asia are also changing fast, though in different ways. Budget airlines are challenging legacy, high-touch airline carriers, while boutique hotels and lifestyle chains offer new trendy and entertaining experiences.

Finally, in the last two chapters of this section, we will take a look at two industries which have experienced fast growth and are likely to continue to do so in Asia: the Asian beauty market with its skincare and cosmetics products as well as new media and purchase outlets such as e-commerce, m-commerce and cloud computing.

15

CONSUMER TECHNOLOGY
THE LANDSCAPE FOR NEW GADGETS

Which Asian consumer technology companies will lead in the new environment?

We all know that Asian consumers love their technology gadgets. Every morning, in buses and trains, we see them quietly sitting and staring at their devices while they process the latest text messages from their friends (full of emoticons), engage in social media, or browse the internet. Asians also must have the latest device: the newest smartphone in their pockets, the latest tablets in their handbags, the latest desktops or laptops at work, and oversized flat-screen TV sets in their homes. It seems that a major part of an Asian consumer's self-identity and pride depends on consumer technology.

Where is the business of consumer technology heading? Which technology companies will lead in the new environment where Asian consumers are using technology devices as lifestyle devices? How important is branding in the technology business?

Stan Shih and the smiling curve

Over the last few years, I have become acquainted and discussed these issues with one of the icons of Asia's high-tech industry: Stan Shih, the founder of Acer, the Taiwanese electronics corporation. After his retirement from Acer, Mr. Shih started the Stans Foundation, an educational venture that offers training and consulting services for Taiwanese executives. He asked me to teach branding courses for the Stans Foundation and to help him set up a Chinese Consumer Center within the foundation.

In 1976, when Stan Shih founded Acer, Taiwan was an assembly line for multinational companies. Many technology companies viewed themselves as original equipment manufacturers (OEMs)—makers of components or equipment on which other companies stick their brand names. Or they ran their business model as original design manufacturers (ODMs) that designed and manufactured entire products, and managed procurement, thus being an outsourced factory for a brand-owning company. Today, more than 90 per cent of global laptop computers are still assembled by Taiwanese ODMs.

ODMs can create their own intellectual property and patent it but they are still a far cry from extracting the added value of a brand.

From the start, while Acer focused its business on being a contract manufacturer (for example, for U.S. companies like IBM), Mr. Shih had also set his mind on building a brand and making Acer a household name. In 2000, he spun off the contract manufacturing division into a separate company, Wistron, and decided to concentrate Acer's consumer electronics operations on its core personal computer (PC) business. Acer established itself as a cost leader, with products generally priced below other branded PCs. The strategy was successful, especially when the PC market became mature. Consumers all over Asia turned to Acer's inexpensive notebooks and netbooks, which constitute 69 per cent of Acer's sales today.

Mr. Shih has become a firm believer in the value of branding. "Innovation is important but today, it's branding that counts," he told me. "If you really want to establish a global brand, you require customer insight. That way you can develop products that are ready for market requirements." By customer insight he means understanding the culture of the consumer. "Culture is daily life. You need an insight into this daily life if you're to tap the huge market we have in Asia. To me, culture is made up of the things you think about, the things you talk about, your behavior. It's taken [Acer] years to develop these kinds of capabilities and this knowledge about the Asian consumer."

Stan Shih is known in Taiwan and mainland China not only as the founder of Acer but also as the creator of the concept of "the smiling curve." The smiling curve, which he first drew on a whiteboard at work in 1992, displays the value-adding potential of different strategies in the technology industry. Both ends of the curve, on the left and on the right, depict higher added value than the middle of the scale: the left end in the form of technological innovation, intellectual property, and R&D know-how, and the right end in terms of branding and

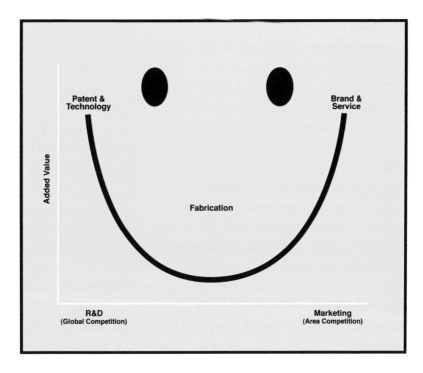

marketing. According to Mr. Shih, the middle of the curve, which represents manufacturing of components and products, requires less knowledge and is less value creating.

Many companies in the technology business have embarked on business strategies aimed at higher value-adding activities. Apple is a good example of an end-to-end value creator. It outsources manufacturing to Taiwanese companies and concentrates on creating value through technical innovation and intellectual property, through devices like iPad and iPod, as well as iTunes and its apps, and through brand and experience management.

Value and value creation, however, are dynamic concepts. What is value creating at one point may be less so at a later stage of development. In the fast-paced business of technology, companies need to ask themselves constantly how they can add new value on the left and right side of the smiling curve. Moreover, the value they create must be in tune with the broader technology ecosystem and be relevant to customers.

It remains to be seen whether Acer has the internal capabilities to add value on both sides of the smiling curve in the new technology environment dominated by the internet and social and mobile media today. One company that has recently failed miserably in value creation, both in terms of developing new relevant technologies as well as marketing and branding, is Sony. On the other side of the coin, a company that has succeeded brilliantly and transformed itself from a low-end manufacturing company to a high-end lifestyle and technology powerhouse is Samsung Electronics.

Samsung's transformation

In the 1990s, Samsung Electronics was a cheap and low-quality maker of consumer electronics products and components. By the late 2000s, Samsung had become the number one or two in many digital categories (LCD television sets, high-memory chips, smartphones, among other products). Organizationally, the company has changed the mindset of its employees from one of purely technical, mechanical, and price considerations to one that includes consumer lifestyle, experience, and emotions.

As part of its transformation, Samsung first engaged in a quality assurance process. To send a clear message to employees that low standards would not be tolerated, some managers staged dramatic events such as burning low-quality products on the factory floor. Next, Samsung improved the design of its products, which traditionally was Sony's turf. Then, it focused on its brand by creating lifestyle products and jazzy ads, and sponsoring major events worldwide such as the Olympics. By the mid-2000s, Samsung wanted to be a creative organization focused on designing new and exciting products for its customers. In line with that, in 2009, they invited me to give a speech on "how to become a love brand." The speaking engagement led me to writing a case study for Columbia Business School and a visit to Samsung's Product Innovation Team (PIT).

PIT started out with one lab in California's Silicon Valley but now has several others, one of them being located in Shanghai. Mr. Yoon Lee, a trained engineer who heads the lab, told me that the "primary mission was to change the consumer-focused development process from being engineering driven to consumer driven." To do so, PIT created a simple process for consumer-driven product development and for gaining insight into customers. PIT's projects resulted in a clear, communicable value proposition for consumers that balanced functional and emotional values. The physical environment at PIT is also quite different—more like Google or an ad agency than a typical Samsung office. The walls are painted with bright primary colors; there is a pool table that stands in one corner; and the surfaces are piled with magazines including fashion, design, and lifestyle magazines. PIT is a clear indication that Samsung is serious about its new focus on the brand, lifestyle, and consumer experience.

Samsung's recent success and its transformation, in all different segments of electronic categories, have been undeniable. Yet, will it continue? Can the company sustain its achievements? Will it also be a leading technology brand in the future? After all, a lot of its past accomplishments were achieved by benchmarking others (first Sony and then Apple). Being the leader at the top is quite different from playing catch-up. It is worthy to note that several technology leaders (such as Nokia and Blackberry) failed miserably just a few years after they had dominated the market.

To be successful in today's environment, what is required is a continuous focus on technology, brands and creativity. In addition, engineering ingenuity must be coupled with a strong consumer focus, and get its employees to concentrate on consumer trends.

Finally, an element of entertainment provides a great experience for consumers. Samsung has greatly benefitted from K-pop and the Korean entertainment wave that has swept Asia from Singapore and Hong Kong to Thailand and Vietnam.

How about Chinese companies?

Besides Samsung, are there other technology makers that may lead in the new technology environment? How about China's Lenovo or Huawei?

Lenovo first entered the global limelight when it acquired IBM's laptop division and its ThinkPad brand in the early 2000s. However, the company faced serious problems soon after, because of cultural challenges following the acquisition, as Deepak Advani, former Chief Marketing Officer, told me. Recently, however, Lenovo has been on a roll, challenging Hewlett-Packard for the number one spot among PC makers in the world. Moreover, Lenovo has a huge market, China, as a home base, and not only for PCs; its mobile phone division is already pitching itself aggressively against Samsung in China.

Lenovo's recent success owes much to a new focused strategy by Yang Yuanqing, its CEO since 2009. In 2009 when Mr. Yang took over, Lenovo posted a loss of USD 226 million; by 2012 the company had doubled its revenues, more than doubled its market share, and had become highly profitable.

Over the last four years, Mr. Yang focused the business on two large profit centers—corporate PC sales and the China market. In addition, Lenovo entered new emerging markets with new products and spent big on promotion, branding, and marketing to create awareness in these markets. In China, Lenovo has built up a vast distribution network and used a similar approach in India. When I visited its headquarters in Beijing, I was impressed by the campus. It is clear that Lenovo is a modern, international organization with a performance culture that adopts English as its official language.

But there are problems on the horizon. Lenovo's recent success is contributed by one market, China, and one dominating category, PCs, which account for 85 per cent of its revenues. Yet, PCs are in the mature stage of the product life cycle and declining fast as a category. Industry sales are shrinking as PCs are becoming obsolete. Consequently, Lenovo needs to add new mobile devices, tablets, and smart television sets to its product categories rapidly, and connect them with "the cloud," in order to remain relevant to Asia's technology-savvy consumers.

Another company to watch is Huawei, based in Shenzhen. Like Lenovo, Huawei has the potential to be a major technology player, but at this point is a question mark as well. The company is the world's second-largest supplier of telecom-network equipment but now wants to build its consumer brand. In 2013, Huawei launched its first global product, a smartphone, to compete with Apple and Samsung.

Will Japan bounce back?

In 2012, NHK, the Japan Broadcasting Corporation, invited me to its program "Global Debate Wisdom" to debate a, by now, perennial topic: the decline of Japan's electronics companies. All the major brands—Sony, Sharp, Toshiba, and Panasonic—had just turned in yet another quarter of dismal performance. What has happened to the country that epitomized Asia's consumer technology industry in the last quarter of the 20th century?

First, Japanese companies kept too many low-value activities (the bottom of the smiling curve) in Japan, known for its high labor costs. Second, while Japanese companies remained innovative, they did not always focus on the right technologies—those needed to compete successfully in the internet and new media age (the left side of the smiling curve). Finally, their marketing and branding have not moved beyond the design focus (the right side of the smiling curve), and do not seem to have the right look and feel or appeal to consumers.

Japanese technology companies are addressing their problems, in part, by outsourcing production, forming joint ventures, and selling unprofitable units. The benefactors are companies in other Asian markets, mostly in Taiwan, mainland China, and South Korea. But Japanese companies also need to create new value, and, most importantly, be more consumer-centric. They must reinvigorate their dormant brands by becoming relevant to today's consumers' lifestyles.

A shift in mindset

The picture that emerges is that technology know-how and R&D are no longer enough for a technology company. Many consumer technology products are as much lifestyle devices these days as they are technology gadgets. While a hard-core engineering orientation may be beneficial, and Asian companies excel at it, such an orientation must be paired with a marketing and branding mindset, and, most importantly, a consumer focus. For many Asian technology companies, this requires the type of internal cultural transformation that Samsung is currently undergoing. The key point seems to be: Don't lose your strengths (such as engineering) but add new skills to it (branding and customer focus). To build these skills, an organization must be focused on marketing innovation (not just technological innovation) and gain in-depth insights on consumers.

Assuming such a shift in mindset and cultural transformation will occur over the next decade in various Asian technology companies, will it come to fruition in products besides computing devices, smartphones, television sets, digital cameras, and camcorders? How about home appliances? How about cars?

Arguably, in both the home appliances and car industries, at this present moment Asian brands don't carry a lifestyle image. In appliances, it is hard to think of any true lifestyle brand anywhere in the world. So, Samsung is trying hard to move into this space with high-tech, well-designed refrigerators, washing machines, microwave ovens, dishwashers, and the like. Cars, on the other hand, do present a lifestyle image, especially at the luxury end, but they are all German (Audi, BMW, and Mercedes) and not Asian brands. However, the German dominance in this sector may not continue in the long term. When I speak to German car executives, they all seem worried and greatly concerned about the low-end makers: ultra-cheap cars coming out of India and China.

I would not be surprised, however, if within a decade or two we would see a luxury lifestyle vehicle coming out of Korea or China, similar to Toyota's Lexus in the United States more than 20 years ago. This is becoming more and more likely as traditional car technology is increasingly merged with consumer electronics. A consumer-centric revolution in the consumer technology industry in Asia may therefore have rippling effects on the car and other industries, and beyond Asia as well.

16

APPAREL AND LIFESTYLE

WILL THERE EVER BE A SUCCESSFUL ASIAN FASHION BRAND?

Asian consumers are obsessed with Western fashion and lifestyle brands although some alternatives (like Shanghai Tang) are emerging

When will we finally see a globally successful Asian fashion brand?

Wait a moment—how about Kenzo, Issey Miyake, and Yohji Yamamoto? Or Uniqlo? Sure … but aside from these Japanese brands, none of the Asian fashion or lifestyle brands has turned into a global success story. None of them—no Chinese, no Indian, no Thai, no Korean brand.

When I travel in Asia, I see a lot of style and excitement in the streets. I see young women and men dressed in the latest fashion outfits. This is a place where consumers love fashion, follow the latest trends, and are not shy to show off their wardrobe. But it is Western brands that fascinate them: Gucci and Prada, Chanel and Dior, Zara and H&M, Coach and Louis Vuitton. They have created retail empires in Tokyo, Hong Kong, and Shanghai.

A report by the World Luxury Association lists the following ten most valuable luxury fashion brands in China: Dior, Chanel, Fendi, Ermenegildo Zegna, Hermes, Louis Vuitton, Ferragamo, Versace, Georgio Armani, and Prada. The same association also compiled lists for private jets, yachts, cars, watches, and jewelry. Western brands dominate all of these categories.

A Chinese-inspired clothing and lifestyle brand

Twenty years ago, in 1994, a Hong Kong businessman set out to change all this. He intended to put China on the map and Chinese-inspired fashion and lifestyle products on the retail shelves. "China's rising, and so should Chinese-style fashion," Sir David Tang was quoted as saying in the 1990s. He created Shanghai Tang and opened a flagship store on Pedder Street in Hong Kong's Central district.

Shanghai Tang is arguably the most comprehensive Chinese-inspired fashion and lifestyle brand today. As such, it might be considered the first global Chinese luxury brand. In 1998, just a few years after Mr. Tang had started the business, he sold his controlling stake to Switzerland-based luxury goods holding company Richemont, one of the three largest luxury goods companies in the world. Shanghai Tang is the one Asian luxury brand in Richemont's portfolio among European fashion brands including Alfred Dunhill, Cartier, Chloé, IWC, and Montblanc, among others.

Yet, growth of the brand has been slow, and at times bumpy. Furthermore, it is hard to imagine that Shanghai Tang would appear on a list of the top global luxury brands. It is therefore not clear whether Shanghai Tang can count as a success story. It is still, by and large, a work in progress.

Mr. Tang is somewhat of a modern Eastern renaissance man. Besides being a designer, he is a restaurateur, Cuban cigar distributor, honorary consul (of Cuba in Hong Kong), columnist, and art collector. He also founded China Clubs in Hong Kong, Singapore, and Beijing. When he gave a talk to a group of Columbia Business School students as part of a student trip to China in the late 1990s, which I attended as the faculty advisor, he spoke more about art and architecture than business.

Mr. Tang has put the imprint of his taste on most of his ventures. Shanghai Tang, with its Mandarin-collared shirts, cheongsam dresses and other Chinese-style fashion, is the most direct expression of his style. Most of the clothing does not appeal to me but I do love the "über-kitschy" Mao-pop-art cufflinks that I purchased in the late 1990s. To me, they are a playful, critical commentary of the contemporary Chinese art movement at the time ("Mao meets Warhol"), and I consider them a contemporary classic.

Perhaps there are others who behave like me. They may pick up an item or two but never become attached to the brand. The brand gained traction early on among aficionados of Chinese cultural styles in the West—mostly tourists who wanted to bring a piece of China back home to the United States, Europe, and Latin America. But this wasn't enough to sustain stores in the West. A couple of years after Shanghai Tang had opened a massive flagship store on Madison Avenue in New York, the store closed due to poor sales. Recently, Shanghai Tang also gave up its Peddar Street flagship store, because the rent was too high.

Most importantly, the brand does not seem to be very popular among Asian consumers, and, in particular, those from Greater China (mainland Chinese, Hong Kongese, Taiwanese, and Singaporeans). They simply don't care much about the brand. As a result, Shanghai Tang's image is that of an obscurity: revered by Western tourists, but not taken seriously as a comprehensive lifestyle brand by a broader segment of Western luxury customers and by Asian consumers, the future luxury buyers.

A second chance

Recently, Richemont appears to have given the brand a second chance and seems to think that it could grow significantly. The company appears to pursue a two-pronged strategy: make the brand famous as a lifestyle brand in the West and, at the same time, attract Asian consumers.

The brand has expanded its store presence significantly over the last five years. Today, Shanghai Tang has stores in major cities outside East Asia—in New York, London, Frankfurt, Moscow, and Dubai. There are also stores in major Asian cities including Hong Kong, Macau, Singapore, and Kuala Lumpur. At the time of this book's writing, the company planned to open a store in Paris and to re-open its store in Tokyo. The company has aggressive expansion plans for China, too. It already has stores in several first- and second-tier cities in China—including several in Beijing and Shanghai, as well as in Guangzhou, Kunming, Shenyang, Xiamen, and Chengdu.

The new stores sport a stylish museum-like Chinese atmosphere. The lighting and merchandise come in typical traditional Chinese colors. The home and gifts collection (the title of the catalogue is "Re-Orient your life") was designed to celebrate the facets of China's past, present, and future. The store is replete with pricey retro China decor, jewelry, and home and dining items, such as Ruyi and Gourd vases in fine bone China, Dragon leather pens, Laughing Buddha bookends, Double Happiness jewelry boxes, Ming vase cushions, Chinese Knot button napkin rings, and Chinese Zodiac chopsticks.

Re-orientation in Shanghai

Positive results are showing. The company reports that the proportion of Shanghai Tang customers from mainland China buying at the boutique's 42 locations worldwide grew to 18 per cent from 2 per cent the same time three years ago. Richemont expects this number to surpass the sales contribution from U.S. customers, at about 22 per cent, very soon.

Still, Shanghai Tang is at a crossroads. It remains to be seen if the new and aggressive investment in the brand will pay off. There have been other attempts to establish a Chinese-inspired luxury fashion brand as a global player, for example, NeTiger, but none has fully made it yet. In addition, in a shopping mall such as Xin Tian Di Style in Shanghai, there are numerous new Chinese brands on display. But in style they are mostly knock-offs of international labels. Shamelessly, they charge similar prices as the original brands that they copy. They try to fool Chinese consumers but are unlikely to ever be successful on an international scale.

Asian fashion models on the rise

Godfrey Gao considers himself a lucky man. The first male Asian supermodel, he has become the first Asian face to front Louis Vuitton's global campaign in the company's 157-year history—one measure of a subtle shift away from Western branding.

"When I got the campaign in 2011 there had been some research into luxury branding and Louis Vuitton was the top brand for Asian consumers, and I think that is the reason why they needed an Asian face," he says. Also, a casual stroll down the Champs-Elysées in Paris is evidence enough, he thinks, that Asian consumers have arrived: "When I was in Paris, I wanted to go and check out the Louis Vuitton store on the Champs-Elysées and, actually, I couldn't even get in," he says. "There was a line from here to the other block—most of them are Chinese." Indeed, 60 per cent of the luxury spending of the Chinese occurs outside the country.

Mr. Gao has numerous female companions. More and more Asian models are appearing in luxury advertisements, abroad and in Asia. The Chinese edition of Vogue and other fashion magazines, in its 500 pages, features a mix of Chinese and Western models, with Chinese models actually dominating. On the top 50 list of the website www.models.com, in 2013 there are five Chinese, one Korean, and one Japanese model. Even if there won't be a globally successful Asian fashion and lifestyle brand, Western brands seem determined to fill in the gap of Asian imagery for Asian consumers.

Copying or leading?

New York Times op-ed columnist David Brooks simply feels that Americans are much better at branding. Branding, in particular the fashion and lifestyle arena, requires creativity, irreverence, and a rebellious spirit—traits that are missing or suppressed in many in Asian societies. Instead, there is just copying of Western brands and marketing approaches. Indeed, many young Asians studying at fashion schools around the world just mimic Western styles, rather than connect with their traditions and invent new expressions. But it is also the Asian consumer: until they show the confidence to give Asian labels a try, to display Asian style, and to immerse themselves in the Asian lifestyle, western brands will still be leading.

Thus, we will have to wait and see whether there will be a successful Asian fashion and lifestyle brand any time soon. In the meantime, Western brands are gradually becoming more Asian by adding Asian elements into their products, store designs, and advertising.

17

FMCGs

THE MASTER IN INSTANT NOODLES AND BEVERAGES

Asia is becoming the battle ground for fast moving consumer goods (FMCGs). As the century of the Asian consumer progresses, Pepsi and Coca-Cola have a new rival who first made it with instant noodles

Walk into any kitchen in an Asian home and you will find instant noodles of different flavors—spicy black pepper, BBQ chicken, miso, curry, kimchi, tom yam, mayonnaise mustard, seafood, the list goes on—stocked up on their shelves. Asian families are crazy over their instant noodles; it's a "must have" item in their food pantries.

Cheap to produce, cheap to purchase, transportable, and convenient, instant noodles are one of Asia's most ubiquitous foods. While instant noodles were created first in 1958 by Japan's Nissin Foods, the leader in China today is not a Japanese company. Taiwan's Wei Ying-Chiao, Chairman of the Ting Hsin International Group, has built an instant noodles empire with his family in mainland China. In the first half of 2012 alone, the company had sales of more than USD 2.5 billion.

Sweet, salty, sour, spicy

Ting Hsin's Master Kong brand, with its chubby fat chef logo, is one of the most recognizable brands in mainland China. When I spoke with Mr. Wei, I quickly understood that taking local food preferences into account was essential for market success. Although the business was already quite successful in Taiwan, the taste, weight, and packaging of instant noodles had to be adjusted when the company entered mainland China. There is a Chinese proverb that says that the flavors are "sweet in the South, salty in the North, sour in the East and spicy in the West." Based on this culinary cultural insight, Mr. Wei told me, "We've segmented this market of 1.3 billion people into seven zones (northeast, northwest, northern China, central China, eastern China, southern China, and the southwest) and we actively developed our branding, adjusting to the particular tastes of each region."

The brand started in a serendipitous fashion. "I once went to Inner Mongolia for a business trip by train, and I ate the instant noodles that I had brought with me from Taiwan in the train. The whole carriage was full of the delicious smell of the noodles and it attracted all the passengers. After that, I was inspired! As soon as we first launched our instant noodles, our product became an instant hit and became highly popular all over China, with demand outstripping supply!"

Indeed, the brand has succeeded beyond expectations: Master Kong Instant Noodles has a 57 per cent share of the Chinese market while the second, third, and fourth players combined have only 33 per cent share.

Tea, fruit juice, and soda

Master Kong is the iconic leader not only in instant noodles. In the late 2000s, Master Kong beverages outperformed both Coke and Pepsi in the ready-to-drink tea market with a market share of about 48 per cent. Moreover, in the fruit juice market (Chinese love orange juice, for example), the company had a market share of 30 per cent, whereas Coca-Cola's Minute Maid and Pepsi's Tropicana are secondary followers offering mostly traditional tropical blends. Coca-Cola still dominates the Chinese soft drink market with a more than 50 per cent market share. But Coca-Cola has not been able to repeat its success with other beverages. Moreover, in 2012, Ting Hsin International took over Pepsi in China, gaining access to 24 bottling factories and gaining the marketing rights for Pepsi's soft drink, juices, and sports drink line. It immediately surpassed Coca-Cola's overall performance. Thus, in the future, one of Coca-Cola's key competitors in China will be Ting Hsin.

There will likely be more to come. *The Financial Times* reports that teas and fruit juices grow twice as fast in Asia as compared to sodas. It is conceivable that in a couple of decades, neither Coca-Cola nor Pepsi may be the largest companies in the non-alcoholic beverage market globally. It may be a little-known company like Ting Hsin, founded in 1991. Indeed, Forbes cited Mr. Wei saying in 2008 that the company would overtake Coca-Cola as the world's largest beverage maker by 2015. We shall wait and see. But the next few years will be decisive.

Building a larger empire

It should be noted that Ting Hsin also has other convenience food brands and other food businesses such as Wei Chuan Food, Ding Sheng, and Bread Societé. In the field of distribution, they own Family Mart convenience stores and Matsusei supermarkets. In the restaurant business, they have a Western fast food chain and Master Kong Chef Table. In the food oils industry, they own Ting Feng, Ting Zheng, and Bing Hsin. Additionally, the Wei family owns the Dicos fried chicken chain, which has more than 1,200 stores in mainland China.

Finally, Ting Hsin's other business interests are in real estate in mainland China and Taiwan, including the iconic Taipei 101, one of the world's tallest buildings. The building has significant retail and dining spaces. When I met Mr. Wei in Taiwan, he hosted dinner for me in one of Taipei 101's restaurants, and told me of the spectacular annual fireworks and displays on the building.

So what's the organizational recipe for Ting Hsin's success? "Our company is run by four brothers, and the four of us cooperate closely and share the same vision," Mr. Wei told me. "The older brother is like the father, a friend to the younger brothers, and the younger brothers respect the elder brothers. We can work tightly together, and achieve a lot through teamwork and synergy. We value honesty, pragmatism, and innovation; and combined with perfect timing, a welcoming environment, and valuing our human resources, Ting Hsin has achieved great fortune." The Ting Hsin success story proves that it no doubt helps to be focused, to work tightly together toward a common goal, and to be ready to plunge when opportunities arise.

It remains to be seen, however, whether a food company like Ting Hsin or, more generally, a fast-moving consumer goods (FMCG) company that is based in greater China could be successful on a global scale. Even other major markets in Asia may be a question mark.

Consider India, the country has a total estimated market size of USD 33 billion by 2015. It has a thriving middle class as well. The market is dominated, however, by several U.S. and Europe-based giants such as Coca-Cola and PepsiCo, Unilever and Procter & Gamble, Kraft, Mars, Kellogg's, Johnson & Johnson, and some local Indian firms. A Chinese company would need to understand the preferences of Indian consumers while competing with experienced players in the industry. Thus, as the century of the Asian consumer progresses, in the FMCG business we may see new powerful regional players such as Ting Hsin that may diminish the market shares of global players, but no new global players of reach comparable to that of the incumbents.

18

THE AIRLINE BUSINESS
TRAVEL ON THE CHEAP

Budget airlines are challenging Asia's legacy airlines. And Asian consumers love it

Singapore Airlines, Cathay Pacific, Thai Airways, All Nippon Airways, Korean Air, and other Asian carriers are revered worldwide for their excellent service, and gracious flight attendants, and gourmet meals offered at a premium price. The tangible and iconic symbol of this type of Asian travel service is Singapore Airlines' flight attendant (originally called "the Singapore Girl"), earning its own wax model in Madame Tussauds in London.

Yet, from almost none a decade ago, the region now has more than 50 budget carriers such as AirAsia. Lion Air, Tiger Airways, Jetstar, and a large number of other startups. These airlines offer air tickets at a low price, with no frills, and are positioned at the exact opposite of the spectrum. The fast growth of these budget airlines clearly indicate a surging demand among Asian consumers for affordable, discounted airline travel.

Never the same again

While budget airlines took off only recently, they are already revolutionizing air travel in Asia, by offering an alternative to the entrenched ways of running the airline business in Asia. The rise of budget airlines follows similar expansions in Europe and North America in previous decades. What People's Express and Southwest Airlines were in the 1980s in the United States, and what Ryanair and EasyJet were in the 1990s in Europe, is now AirAsia and Jetstar in Asia.

According to CWT Travel Management Institute, the share of the Asian aviation market enjoyed by low-cost carriers surged from zero to 20 per cent in 2012. This share is still lower than in the United States (30 per cent), Latin America (31 per cent), and Europe, Middle East, and Africa (36 per cent). But in Asia, the industry is currently growing 5 per cent compared to less than 1 per cent growth in the other regions. And the party has just begun. Asia's budget carriers seem to be at the beginning of the rapid growth path experienced earlier by the budget carriers in the United States, Europe and elsewhere.

At the time of this book's writing in early 2013, there are more than 1,000 aircraft on order. Lion Air's co-founder Rusdi Kirana placed an unprecedented order of 230 Boeing planes in 2012 and ordered 234 medium-haul aircraft from Airbus in early 2013. The total number of budget airlines in Asia was estimated to grow to more than 60 by 2015. Futhermore, the established airlines were rushing into the budget airline business. Thai Airways had Nok Air and Thai Smile; Singapore Airlines launched Scoot. China's Eastern Airlines Co. entered into a joint venture with Australian airline Qantas' subsidiary Jetstar, with a budget carrier out of Hong Kong. Malaysia and Singapore had built budget terminals back in 2006 and both were expanding these budget terminals. Around one-third of travelers going through Singapore were budget travelers. It was expected that by 2015 carriers in Asia would be able to enjoy more growth, as ASEAN's open skies agreement would be finalized by then, allowing airlines to access new markets with the liberalization of airspace between member countries.

They said, "It will never work"

Not long ago, airline executives stated that low-cost carrier operations wouldn't work in Asia. After all, budget airlines seemed like buses—a mode of transportation that Asians don't particularly like. Budget airlines transport you to a destination with minimum degree of comfort. All you get is a small seat, limited check-in baggage, and you have to bring your own food, or else you pay high prices for it. This lack of service and functional treatment wouldn't fit the Asian psyche.

They were wrong. The success of the budget airlines is, in fact, closely linked to a key characteristic of the Asian consumers: looking for value. Having a gourmet meal served to you at eye-level-service by a gracious Asian host or hostess at a premium price may seem valuable if you are on an expense account, but what if you have to pay on your own, or if you travel on vacation with your family? You can probably do without these frills on a two- to four-hour flight.

Moreover, with the fast-rising middle class, the size and competition of the market have changed and new segments have entered the market. Instead of having full-service travel, some of these customers are looking for cheaper fares and access to formerly underserved destinations in the region, which the established airlines found not profitable due to high operational costs.

The benefits of the rise of budget airlines for Asian consumers are thus obvious: more choice. Furthermore, it turns out that budget airline travel is not only for leisure travelers on vacation. It is also for passengers on business trips. Because of their collectivist nature, Asians prefer to do business face-to-face, and that doesn't mean screen-to-screen. They like to meet their counterparts frequently, talk, and entertain. Often business is done in close-by, smaller cities; that's where people in your "in-group" are located and where you can leverage your relationships. But the smaller cities are not where legacy airlines want to fly. Low-cost air carriers that offer such unusual destinations are the alternative, and they may even include smaller, fast-developing destinations (remember, the rise of the middle class is not only in the major cities!) where legacy airlines do not traditionally fly to.

Asia thus has all the factors for discount airlines to thrive: a growing middle class, large populations in less-than-three-hour flights, and a lower middle class that may be eager to travel for the first time, or an upper middle class that goes on weekend vacation trips.

When China awakes, the skies will shake

There has been one market in Asia, and one group of consumers, that have been entirely isolated from the budget airline boom thus far. It is the biggest market of all: China. Just imagine what will happen when budget carriers are allowed to enter the Chinese market. Their prices will surely drop drastically as in the other markets, and demand for airline travel will likely rise rapidly.

The Chinese government therefore keeps tight control over the rapidly growing airline industry, by making it hard to start a new airline and secure routes. It thus protects the three big state-owned carriers that dominate the market: Beijing-based Air China Ltd., Shanghai-based China Eastern Airlines Corp. and Guangzhou-based China Southern Airlines Ltd. It also wants to prevent the industry from growing too fast and compromising safety. In fact, China would not have enough airports of adequate size to handle a booming budget airlines market.

With close to 250 million passengers a year, according to the Civil Aviation Authority of China, China's domestic market is already huge. In 2011, the three big state-owned airlines carried 191 million passengers; the rest of the market was served by some private operators and some smaller airlines, in part owned by the big three.

But the forecast is that the market will grow six-fold by 2030. China is building 82 new airports and renovating 101 others in a five-year plan that runs until 2015. And Chinese carriers are exploring the budget idea. When I conducted a workshop for China Eastern Airlines in the spring of 2013, we had a discussion on the aforementioned launch of a budget subsidiary, together with Qantas out of Hong Kong.

New airports needed, in China and elsewhere

Tough business

Yet, the future isn't entirely rosy for Asian budget operators. The extremely tight operating margins that exist in the budget airline business are an obstacle, especially for smaller budget airlines. Many of the low-cost carriers are just barely profitable despite rising traffic, reflecting the intense competition. Round-trip tickets on the popular Singapore–Kuala Lumpur route are as low as USD 43, compared with USD 250 on a premium airline and about USD 100 on a luxury bus ride.

Thus, a consolidation of the market seems to be on the horizon. Any new upstart must strive to be big really fast, or be doomed. Some budget airlines already sell tickets way below break-even prices, even in the big markets. Take Indonesia. It has had growth rates only slightly behind China over the last decade, yet two of its budget airlines ran into financial problems. One of them, Batavia Air, was even forced to declare bankruptcy. The verdict seems to be that bigger budget airlines will get bigger, and smaller ones will find it hard to survive.

Thus, Asia's budget airlines are seeking to boost revenues through ancillary income to drive profitability. Ancillary income includes charges for additional baggage, food, special seats, flight changes, merchandise, and creative services (like loaning iPads or videogames).

Are budget airlines a major threat?

Established carriers clearly offer a better product in terms of service, convenient scheduling, and reliability. The industry is also still growing. Yet, could low-cost carriers, especially the big survivors that emerge after a market consolidation, ultimately topple legacy airlines? From talking to airline executives, I know that they are concerned, although they consider this to be an issue in the distant future. Based on the recent developments in the Asian airline industry, though, I wonder what "distant future" might mean. Ten years, perhaps?

Because of the perceived threat, many full-service carriers have decided to start their own budget airline to protect their own turf and reach out to new customer segments. One strategy is to develop their own routes and offer it to their low-cost subsidiary. Full-service airlines have also learned some new tricks from budget airlines, for example, by charging extra for ancillary services.

Clearly, legacy airlines face a new reality—one that was unimaginable as recently as ten years ago. The future will call for cost efficiencies and profit maximization while not compromising the quality of customer service. It will call for a multipronged strategy, having more alliance networks and subsidiaries that include budget airlines. Most importantly, it will call for in-depth customer insight and segmenting the Asian travel market in new ways, for example, by lifestyle rather than by the traditional first-, business-, and economy-class categories.

19

HOSPITALITY
ARE ASIANS READY FOR TRENDY HOTELS?

Boutique hotels provide lifestyle alternatives to traditional high-end hotels. But the incumbents are reacting

Like airlines, the hotel market in Asia is experiencing a new consumer trend. If the new development in the hotel sector may not be as noticeable and far-reaching yet as the low-cost revolution in the airline sector, it will have major repercussions in the industry in due time. The trend, in this case, however, is not price focused. It is not about saving money. It is about another consumer trend: experience and lifestyle.

Hotels in Asia generally are of excellent quality, especially the five-star hotels. These upscale and luxury hotels traditionally feature a wide range of services and amenities (multiple restaurants and bars, elaborate fitness centers, business and concierge services), large rooms, premier locations, and Asian-style service. They tend to cater specifically to business travelers. They are part of international chains (such as Hilton, Hyatt, Intercontinental, Marriott, Sheraton, and the like) or largely regional hotel brands (such as the Mandarin Oriental headquartered in Hong Kong, the Shangri-La based in Singapore, or the Taj Hotels in India). Over the last 20 years, I have stayed in many such properties all across Asia. In my view, they are the best in the world, exceeding by far hotels in other parts of the world. I have a couple of relative favorites in each city that I visit, and a few absolute favorites such as the Kowloon Shangri-La, the first such hotel I ever stayed in during my first trip to Asia in 1991. Back then, it was featured as one of the best hotels in Hong Kong. That may no longer be the case. But the service remains attentive; the views of Hong Kong Harbor are spectacular; the lobby is the right scale; and the hotel has taken on a patina of elegance, which I adore.

While these traditional five-star hotels offer wonderful facilities and services, they also share a common approach and are not well differentiated. They have similar designs: either some Asian interpretation of the French Ancien Régime aesthetics or bland-contemporary. They also have similar services and facilities. Most importantly, they are not "cool" and trendy.

Thus, over the last few years, a growing segment of business travelers have grown tired of staying in these impersonal, faceless hotels. They are looking to stay at properties that are different, less mass market, and more intimate. They are looking for hotels that surprise them and offer them an experience.

Enter the boutique hotels

In Asia and elsewhere, boutique hotels are typically small, stand-alone hotels (such as Upper House in Hong Kong, Tenface in Bangkok, or The Courtyard in Kuala Lumpur) or small local chains (like the Tango in Taiwan). In some cities, boutique hotels are spreading like mushrooms: in Shanghai there is Pudi Boutique Hotel, Jia Hotel, 88 Xintiandi, Puli, URBN Hotel, and the Waterhouse at South Bund, with its über-cool warehouse-cum-military chic, to name but a few.

Boutique hotels are usually design-thematic (minimalist, retro, or contemporary-futuristic) or content-thematic (inspired by location, culture, or history). They are multisensory— all about looks, textures, smells, and sound. Music seems omnipresent. They have attention-grabbing architecture and interior design. The lobby and guest rooms make a statement.

The prime target of boutique hotels is the discerning business traveler who works hard and plays hard. Simultaneously, the boutique hotels appeal to the trendy leisure traveler.

To get the feel of a particular boutique hotel, I recommend browsing the web site first: you immediately sense how the hotel wants to be different. For example, The Tango, where I stayed a couple of times, promises a mix of taste, fashion, slowness, style, and calmness. Here is what they mean by each term, as explained on their web site:

- *Taste: The combination of sensibility and rationality*
- *Fashion: Immerse yourself in grace and elegance*
- *Slowness: The enjoyment of slow-paced life*
- *Style: Be the very you*
- *Calmness: Low-key but luxurious*

Do you get it? Well, I did not understand it completely when I browsed the site for the first time. Illustrating each concept with an image helped but one really has to stay in a boutique hotel to get a full impression. Here is what I remember about my Tango experience: the trendy dress code of the service staff; the very dark look of the entire hotel (a frequently used style in boutique hotels); a huge water pipe running straight into the round bathtub, which was situated adjacent to the small and dark living room and workspace. When I stay in a standard five-star hotel, my memory of it is usually much less vivid. You see, boutique hotels are all about memorable and unforgettable experiences!

The Tango is a small local chain (they currently have five hotels only). However, there is also a boutique hotel chain (they prefer the term "lifestyle brand") that is part of Starwood, a large hotel conglomerate. Named W Hotels Worldwide (or, in short, "the W"), it is aggressively expanding globally, particularly in Asia.

Wordwide Wow. Now.

The W is considered the most successful hotel launch in recent years. It was developed in 1998 by former Starwood founder and CEO, Barry Sternlicht, a visionary hotelier. As I am writing this, there are W Hotels in Bangkok, Guangzhou, Hong Kong, Seoul, Singapore, Shanghai, and Taipei, and W Retreats in Bali, the Maldives, and Koh Samui. They plan to have four additional properties in China, one additional property in Indonesia, four in India, one in Macau, and one in Kuala Lumpur over the next five years. The management of the W certainly seems confident that Asians are ready for boutique hotels.

The W is a lifestyle destination. Although it is a chain hotel, the W is fun. Here is a description from its web site:

> Escape to where iconic design and contemporary luxury set the stage for exclusive and extraordinary experiences at W Hotels® Worldwide. Retreat to surprising, sensory environments where amplified entertainment, vibrant lounges, modern guestrooms and innovative cocktails and cuisine create more than just a hotel experience, but a luxury lifestyle destination.

The W experience is branded as "Worldwide Wow. Now." In addition, there are sub-brands, for example, the W Pillow Menu ("Choose between a body pillow, neck roll, firm foam PrimaLoft pillow or 100 per cent goose-down feather pillow."). W's signature service is trademarked as Whatever/Whenever™ ("Whatever you want. Whenever you want it."). Then there is PAW ("Pets are Welcome— We've created a special program to make your pet's experience as wonderful as yours."). The fitness club is called SWEAT™ ("From elliptical cross trainers, free weights and high-tech machines to personal training, Pilates and yoga, Sweat is your state-of-the-art way to stay fit.").

The W experience is about feeling good and being happy. There is always a stylish decor, a great bar with beautiful people, and young, enthusiastic staff. Increasingly, the W also seems to think of itself as a multimedia company. There are collaborations with filmmakers, fashion designers, and media companies. Together with Intel, the W launched short films on YouTube. At the Singapore, Bangkok, and Shanghai properties, they are holding an exclusive photo retrospective of Madonna, the American singer, songwriter, and entertainer.

Yet, some think all of this may be too much—"overdesigned," "too cool for its own sake," "a party place from the West with little soul implanted into Asia," "too much Wow and hedonistic overkill!" When I visited the W Singapore with a group of executive students in 2013 as part of my course on Asian consumer insight, the group seemed divided. Some loved it; others preferred the more traditional hotel that we visited the next day.

Time will tell whether Asians are ready for the type of coolness and "worldwide wow now" exemplified by the W and other boutique hotels. There is a danger: hype and crash. As with many other fads in Asia, the W and boutique hotels may become all the rage for a few years, and then go out of style. However, right now, established players view the W and, more generally, boutique hotels, as a potential threat, and they wonder whether a tidal change may be coming.

How to react?

The obvious response to the threat posed by the boutique and lifestyle brands may be to enrich one's own product by adding new features and improving service. Thus, established players in the hospitality industry are updating and upgrading their facilities more frequently, providing more convenient check-in and check-out options, expanding their "frequent guests" programs, and offering additional food and beverage options.

Customers welcome such initiatives. They appeal to the value-driven, functional, and traditional mentality of Asian consumers. They are also in line with some of the trends among Asian luxury travelers such as increasing interest in food and wine, high level of comfort, personalized services, and digital technologies, observed by hospitality market research firms. But they are reactive rather than innovative. They are intended to lure the existing customer base of travelers with more of the same rather than excite them with something new. They may not go far enough to rebuff the new entrants.

Some hotel chains have chosen a more aggressive approach: they have launched their own boutique hotel chain. To avoid cannibalization of its customers, they have done so under a new separate name, and not under the existing five-star hotel name, or as a line extension. International hotel conglomerates primarily seem to pursue this route. Sensing that it was an attack against the W, Starwood was initially successful in fighting off a Hilton boutique chain launch called Denizon in the U.S. courts by suing Hilton for stealing documents. But the glare may only last for a while. Hilton may launch a new chain with a new name and concept. Another competitor, the Intercontinental Hotel Group (IHG), has done exactly that already. The first hotel in Asia of its new Indigo chain is a 180-room property located on the riverfront Bund in Shanghai, launched in 2010 as part of the Shanghai World Expo. Indigo now has five hotels in China and plans to open hotels in key Asian cities such as Hong Kong, Singapore, and Tokyo soon. Whether this "jump on the bandwagon" approach will also work for the Asian hotel chains remains to be seen. It is not clear whether the Mandarin Oriental, Shangri-La, or Taj Hotel could, or should, follow suit.

Besides updating and upgrading, or following the trend, there is a third way: to reposition and focus a hotel on Asian lifestyles. Consider one of the current lifestyle trends: health and wellness. Asian travelers in general and younger generations, in particular, are increasingly concerned about health, and engage in fitness, weight balance, and general well-being programs. Health is of concern to Asians because they are witnessing new challenges to their health due to rapid economic development (think: stress and air pollution). Keeping fit and managing one's weight have health benefits and also produce the toned body look and shape promoted in fashion and lifestyle media. Furthermore, general well-being seems to be a physical and spiritual imperative to guaranteeing a satisfying and happy life.

To help their guests with their wellness management, many hotels have vastly expanded their fitness clubs and spas. In fact, some

Asian hotel chains are entirely positioned as wellness and spa havens. Banyan Tree Hotels and Resorts—a brand that began with one resort in Phuket in 1994 but now has 30 hotel properties and 60 spas—delivers, according to their web site, "rest and relaxation to the world weary" and a "sanctuary for the senses."

The Asian tropical spa

A major innovation of the company was the concept of the Asian tropical spa. When I met with Ho Kwon Ping, founder and Executive Chairman of Banyan Tree, he told me that, before launching the spa concept, he had brought in consultants from Europe who advised him against creating a spa in Southeast Asia. The consultants said that the natural conditions for a spa were not present: there are neither cold climates nor hot springs in Southeast Asia, and spas are not associated with the medical image (face masks and quasi-medical treatments), which are common in Europe. Mr. Ho decided to ignore their advice and went ahead to create an Asian spa concept, which he has now successfully implemented globally. "We brought in tropical flora. We created all kinds of spa oils from everything that was available in Asian culture, in Thai culture. We created all these Asian-type therapies. And now every single spa in Asia has a tropical resort spa," he said. By being distinctly Asian, the Banyan Tree has successfully differentiated itself in Asia and beyond.

Banyan Tree has also capitalized on another mega-trend: the green element and concern for the environment. "The green element and the environment are actually very important because it's part of our fundamental DNA," Mr. Ho said to me. Mr. Ho also cares deeply about corporate social responsibility (CSR). "A resort can totally destroy the physical environment. So many resorts have gone in and destroyed the coral reefs, for example, by having construction mud flowing into the reefs. At the physical level you can destroy a pristine environment. At the social-cultural level, you have a situation where rich tourists come in and pay a room rate in one day that is equal to a month's salary for the staff, so you've got social-economic dislocation too. So tourism, resort tourism, in a social-cultural context, is not all good and not all bad. It has the potential to be both. Tourism, for myself, is a vehicle for trying to implement all the corporate social responsibility things I've wanted to do since I was young." Indeed, Banyan Tree with its green and corporate social responsibility practice has set the stage for other Asian-inspired resorts and spa chains to follow.

In sum, there are different lifestyles and value positioning that established hotels and resorts can use to make their offers more appealing to their Asian guests. It doesn't have to be just traditional Asian-style service alone, or hedonism and fun. An innovative approach may be, in fact, to go back in time to rediscover aspects of Asian cultures and values that are particularly relevant for the savvy Asian lifestyle traveler today.

20

ASIAN BEAUTY
MAKE ME UP

Skincare, cosmeceuticals, plastic surgery – where is the business of beauty heading?

For generations of Asians, female beauty used to be simple: you were either born with it or not. For special occasions (weddings, ceremonies, or family get-togethers), you applied a little bit of make-up. To protect your skin against the elements, you used a simple, natural moisturizer. You washed your hair with soap or a simple shampoo for all hair types.

Beauty isn't that simple anymore. It isn't simple any more for women and is getting harder and harder for the beauty industry. As a female consumer, you are bombarded with images of what it means to be beautiful and how you are supposed to care for your face and body. Looking your best is essential for success in your private and public life. The pressure is huge, and the beauty industry knows it, having created this pressure, in part, through marketing and advertising. The industry thus constantly launches new products that claim to be better, softer, and more effective. Competition in the industry for new beauty concepts and products is intense, among global and Asian firms.

Beauty today manifests itself along various dimensions or, rather, dichotomies and tensions. Beauty can be natural or engineered; it may be seen as outward or coming from within; it may be achieved as an international, global look or as a culturally ingrained, ethnic look; it may be created for the moment or to last; and it is judged by yourself or by others (both men *and* women). Beauty is a complex physical, socio-cultural, and marketing phenomenon. Today Asia is its playground—and battleground.

The Asian skincare market

Growth in Asian beauty markets has outpaced growth in Western markets for years. Over a ten-year period, from 2001 to 2011, there has been double-digit growth in most Asian markets. More importantly, Asian countries such as Japan, Korea, and China are one of the few countries in the world where skincare outsells make-up and cosmetics, and growth in the premium skincare market is particularly strong.

Asian women treat their skin and appearance as a serious endeavor, not as superficial fun; their obsession for clean, clear, flawless skin and skin whitening products has created a huge market. Incidentally, the idea that white skin is highly desirable has a long tradition. During the Han dynasty in China, white skin was already the beauty ideal. Dark skin was associated with poor farmers who worked in the fields. That is why Asia's new middle and upper classes desire white skin; it is not for racial but economic and prestige reasons.

Asian women use numerous skincare products a day. (The frequently quoted number of 5–7 products is outdated!) These products include make-up remover, cleanser, toner, face serum, emulsion, face cream, eye cream, sun care product, and neck cream among others. Add to this the occasional moisturizing pack, deep cleansing mask, eye mask, scrub or peeling treatment, and you've got a fully packed closet of skincare products. In addition, there are the make-up products: face powder, foundation, mascara, eyeliners, nail polish, lipgloss, lipstick, and the occasional multi-tasker (the BB, CC, or DD cream). The product variety is mind-boggling—and rising all the time.

Western firms, such as Estée Lauder and L'Oréal at the premium end, and Unilever and Proctor & Gamble, have made substantial investments in Asia. However, Western skin care and cosmetics products are not quite as welcomed as Western fashion products. Asian women feel that their skin care requirements are different. Indeed, Asian skin does not wrinkle as fast as Caucasian skin, but brown spots emerge much earlier. Moreover, Asians feel that the product line of Western brands often does not display the same variety or the marketing does not appeal to them. As a result, they do not fully trust Western brands.

Let's take a look at the South Korean market— considered the lead market for skincare and cosmetics products in Asia today.

Be serious about how you look

Korean consumers are obsessed with beauty. Many women believe that having the right face makes all the difference between success and failure. Therefore, they are extremely knowledgeable about their products and take their beauty routine very seriously. It is estimated that South Korean women use on average 17 products daily.

As in other Asian markets, skincare products are booming in South Korea. The skincare market grew by 58 per cent from 2005 to 2010. The growth was driven by products with new ingredients and claims of improved performance. Myeong-dong, one of Seoul's busiest shopping districts, has more than 1,000 cosmetics shops and hundreds of skincare stores within a small quadrant alone. Foreign beauty brands are well recognized but they are struggling, even though both Estée Lauder and L'Oréal have tailored their products with unique formulas for the Korean skin.

AmorePacific, South Korea's largest cosmetics and skincare firm, is the leader with a market share of 38 per cent in 2010. About ten years ago, when the skincare boom started to take off, I consulted for AmorePacific on several projects. The company had just given up its Korean name and adopted AmorePacific. One of the projects called for repositioning its highest-share brand, Laneige, from a cosmetics to a natural skincare brand and getting it ready for Asian markets outside Korea. We had known from research that a boom in natural skincare would be coming. Another project was the launch of the AmorePacific flagship brand, carrying the new company name, in South Korea and in the United States. We decided on an experiential positioning focused on two very Asian concepts: balance and energy. Most of the products included natural ingredients, such as seven-year-old red ginseng, green tea, and bamboo shoots, which Western women value, too, for their presumed skin and health benefits.

South Korea's neighbors have come to recognize the country and its manufacturers such as Amore Pacific as innovation leaders. The Laneige brand, for example, nowadays claims significant market shares in other Asian markets. AmorePacific's competitor, LG Household & Health Care, also promotes the Korean concept of beauty to the world. In 2010, it acquired a new chain of natural products stores, The Face Shop, and launched them all across Asia. The Face Shop now has more than 2,000 stores in over 20 countries, and more than 500 stores in Japan and China alone.

The beauty industry in South Korea is not resting on its laurels. It is constantly working on the next "big thing"—not just another product, but an entirely new line of beauty products, or perhaps a fresh concept for a new target market. For example, products for teenagers and even pre-teens were such an idea. Also nowadays, male consumers, too, seem to be concerned about their skin. They feel they need to keep up with women fashion trends and consider it to be fashionable and manly to color their hair, apply BB cream on their skin, and use eyebrow liners. There is no association whatsoever with "gay lifestyle." This is just what a modern man needs to do. Korean manufacturers have therefore introduced several dedicated male skincare brands and

As seen in the trendy Garosu-gil district in Seoul

are promoting them heavily with male idols and actors. As in the women's market, the trend is likely to continue and will result in targeted products for increasingly specific applications.

Natural cosmeceuticals

Another new concept, in South Korea and elsewhere, is "cosmeceuticals." The term "cosmeceuticals" combines the words "cosmetics" and "pharmaceuticals." Whereas cosmetics and skincare products are designed to nourish and beautify in the short run, cosmeceuticals emphasize efficacy and long-term effects. It is claimed that biologically active ingredients in cosmeceuticals have medical skin benefits. Taken orally, they are called "nutricosmetics." Although these products give themselves a medical image, they are not registered as medicine or drugs, and do not need to prove their effectiveness in rigorous scientific testing.

While Western cosmeceuticals pitch themselves as advanced skincare science, Asian products are using their own spin. Among Asian brands, the concept of natural ingredients is predominant, referring to the allegedly proven effects of hundreds of years of Eastern medicine. Thus, Asian brands include Chinese herbal extracts, marine plants, micro-organisms, and even animal organs, extracted through biotechnologies. Bird's nest, for white skin, is one of the classics; bee venom and snail slime are one of the more exotic varieties.

Natural cosmeceuticals are part of a trend all over Asia to combine naturalness with functionality, and tradition with modern technology. In China, the market for traditional Chinese medicine-style beauty products is estimated to be more than USD 1 billion. Since Chinese consumers continue to take traditional Chinese medicine seriously and consider it as being natural and effective (with no side effects), Chinese firms could be well positioned for the future.

Consider, for example, mainland giant Shanghai Jahwa. They launched the Herborist brand described as follows on its web site:

> Herborist uses traditional knowledge from the Chinese herbal science to create its precious products: delicate encounter between traditional knowledge and state-of-the-art contemporary cosmetics science … Plants, like any living being, carry a fundamental inner force. The Chinese have always used this force to balance and circulate energies and thus reach the very essence of beauty.

And the reality is …

While skincare products, as well as herbal cosmeceuticals, may improve your facial appearance slightly in the short term, most products achieve very little in the long term irrespective of how expensive they are. They can fix you up for the moment but they do not change your basic condition. They do not transform you into a stunning physical beauty, not overnight, and not even in a few months or years.

Most aspects of physical beauty—whether you have soft skin, whether you get your first wrinkles at 35 or 45, whether your hair thins early on or later in life, and thus how young or old you look— are genetically determined. Also genetically determined is your skin tone and color of your skin, whether you tend to get blemishes or pimples easily, and whether your hair tends to be dry or oily. Moreover, research in evolutionary psychology has shown that respondents from various cultures and diverse backgrounds prefer symmetrical faces and rank women with a small waist-to-hip ratio (the waist being 70 per cent the size of the hips), irrespective of different weights, as the most attractive. Unfortunately, it seems that you either have it or you don't.

There is a comforting saying that women used to believe in: "Beauty is just skin deep." It means that physical beauty is superficial and that good looks aren't everything. So, why worry about it? Beauty

BEFORE

AFTER

is not the reflection of your character or personality, and character or personality is what really counts. So don't get too hung up about beauty. Recently, the argument has been turned on its head: beauty is not just about looks. It is about character and personality, for example, self-confidence and self-esteem, and everybody can be beautiful. Based on this new view of beauty, it seems that the beauty industry had used a distorted definition of beauty in the past. They had manipulated women with stereotypical images of beauty and portrayed a state of beauty that is not achievable. One player in the industry argued exactly that. Remember Dove's Campaign for Real Beauty? The campaign for this Unilever brand showed ads on YouTube of "real beauty"—ordinary women who weren't perfect by traditional beauty standards.

The campaign was highly successful in some Western markets. But Asian women and the experts (the South Koreans) didn't seem to buy the argument. They saw it as a cheap way out and embarked on a permanent solution to the problem of physical beauty: plastic surgery.

A technologically advanced concept of beauty

South Koreans undergo more plastic surgery than any other nationality: in 2011, 13 million procedures were performed on a population of just 50 million. Some say that the actual figures may be even higher because cash transactions and plastic surgeries in some shopping malls are not included. Plastic surgery includes skin and hair treatments; breast augmentation, fat reduction, and surgery on other parts of the body. Moreover, South Korea is becoming a harbor of plastic surgery for other Asians as well: in 2010, more than 80,000 visitors came to have a medical procedure done. It is projected that by 2015 the visitors coming strictly for medical procedures may reach 400,000, an estimated growth rate of 30 per cent annually.

Facial surgery used to be limited to minor adjustments to noses and eyelids. The new concept of beauty, however, calls for the creation of a entirely new face: an egg-shaped rather than the traditional round Korean face. In the spring of 2013, a Japanese blog, Livedoor, published the faces of 20 Miss Korea contestants, noting their similarities and that "Korea's plastic surgery mayhem is finally converging on the same face." It wasn't clear whether the photos were digitally enhanced, or whether all the women featured were in fact contestants. But the key point seems accurate: the desirable facial look among South Koreans is converging and has diminished the Korean ethnic look.

In a focus group that I conducted with Korean consumers as part of an ACI beauty project, the participants proudly declared that Korea has an advanced view of beauty. Unlike other Asian women (such as Chinese, Indonesians, and Indians) who hold a more cautious view of plastic surgery, South Koreans are excited and confident about plastic surgery. The idea seems to be: why use fix-up products when a permanent solution is available? Or, why not get a permanent, more effective fix and then supplement the new look with skincare products and cosmetics?

Hurrah!!! Finally, here it is. A new and technologically advanced concept of beauty. Korea seems to be prepared to share its new

"Korean wave of beauty" with the rest of the world, just as it did with its Gangnam style rap. Perhaps, as fast as Gangnam style has become the reference for rap music, Korean-style plastic surgery will become the reference point for Asian – and even Western women – across the globe.

21

NEW MEDIA
E-COMMERCE, M-COMMERCE, AND "THE CLOUD"

E-commerce companies such as Alibaba are transforming Asian markets and corporations. But once m-commerce and "the cloud" gain steam, their dominance may be challenged

In its March 23, 2013 issue, *The Economist*, ended its main editorial with a bold prediction about China's largest e-commerce firm: "Alibaba has the potential to become the world's most valuable company." An article in the same issue, titled "The world's greatest bazaar," reinforced this point.

The fact that a magazine like *The Economist* and industry experts are contemplating that Alibaba may become the most valuable company in the world indicates to me that e-commerce, online and mobile platforms have become a major force in China and Asia as a whole.

A transformational company

Alibaba Group is a Hangzhou-based family of internet-based e-commerce businesses that cover business-to-business online marketplaces, retail and payment platforms, shopping search engines, and data-centric cloud computing services. In 2013, Alibaba had 24,000 employees at its Hangzhou headquarters and elsewhere. In September 2012, it was reported that Alibaba had made a profit of USD 485 million on revenues of USD 4.1 billion. By many counts, Alibaba is the world's largest e-commerce company, dominating China's e-commerce market. In 2012, the company handled more transactions than eBay and Amazon combined: a whopping 1.1 trillion yuan (USD 170 billion) in sales. The company is also expanding gradually on a global scale and turning to new products. *The Economists* featured Alibaba as a "transformative company," which changes Chinese business, its markets, and its economy.

At the time of this book's writing, Alibaba was still a private company. In June 2012 its founder, Jack Ma, told a Bloomberg Businessweek reporter that "some day Jack Ma is going to retire—maybe not very long [from now] … Life is so short. I don't want to be 80 years old and still running this company." In 2013, a few months after he had turned 48, he resigned as CEO. This was quite an unusual move for a leader in a region where executives and government officials often stay on as long as the Pope. "Stepping down as CEO is a difficult decision, for this could be confounding especially for someone of my age who should be at the height of his career," he wrote in a letter to his employees, adding "at 48 I am no longer 'young' for the internet business."

With Mr. Ma stepping down as CEO, though staying on as Executive Chairman, and Jonathan Lu Zhaoxi, aged 43, taking over, it was expected that the firm would have its initial public offering (IPO) by the end of 2013 or early 2014.

E-commerce today—and what's coming

Alibaba's success is closely intertwined with the rise of the e-commerce business in China. As China is on its way to becoming the world's biggest economy, its e-commerce market is likely to overtake the United States and other countries. By 2020, China's e-commerce market is forecast to be bigger than the existing markets in the United States, the United Kingdom, Japan, Germany, and France combined.

According to a March 2013 report of the McKinsey Global Institute, e-tailing produced more than USD 190 billion in 2012 sales. China's e-tailing industry has posted 120 per cent compound annual growth since 2003. More than 6 million e-merchants list on Taobao. Singles Day 2012 (a day in November when young Chinese celebrate their bachelor lives) generated USD 4 billion in online sales, surpassing Cyber Monday (the first Monday after Thanksgiving) in the United States.

Moreover, the McKinsey Global Institute predicts strong growth in the business for years to come, pointing out that China's broadband penetration is only 30 per cent. They believe that online sales could reach USD 650 billion by 2020 and lift China's private consumption by an additional four to seven per cent.

Asia as a whole is thus quickly becoming the world's fastest growing and biggest e-commerce market. In 2012, it grew twice as fast as the United States. Asia's direct-to-consumer e-commerce sales grew 25 per cent over the previous year. In its inaugural report on Asia's top 500 retailers, *Internet Retailer*, a portal to e-commerce intelligence, reported that the combined sales of the region's ten largest web retailers (Alibaba, Rakuten, 360Buy.com, Amazon.com, Suning Commerce, Jia.com, eBay, 51Buy.com, HappiGo, and Vancl) accounted for 86 per cent of all the sales of Asia's top 500 retailers.

E-commerce of the future will increasingly take place on mobile platforms. M-commerce grew by more than 200 per cent between 2011 and 2012, according to Chinese research group iiMedia. Similar developments for mobile platforms are occurring in other Asian markets as well, and consumers in some Asian markets have been using them for years. I distinctly remember an incident when I visited Indonesia in the early 2000s for a business seminar in Jakarta. I was sitting in the car with the conference organizer after my speech at the seminar, and he said that he would instantly pay me the second half of my speaking fees. He pulled out his phone, accessed an app from his bank, and—bingo, it was done! At that time in the United States, my clients still mailed me checks through the postal services.

The m-commerce market is only in its early stages. However, rapid growth is expected to happen at any moment. Asian consumers are psychologically hooked on their mobile devices more than their U.S. and European counterparts. Many young Asian consumers have started their communication lives with mobile phones, or even smartphones, rather than land lines or the internet. They are extremely mobile savvy. The smartphone seems to be the center of their lives where they manage their personal relationships and businesses. In addition, Asian consumers are value-conscious, and they know it is online where they will get the best deals.

Finally, due to limitations in the physical infrastructure in rural areas, these Asian consumers will find it harder to get from place to place. As most of them do not own a car, shopping is definitely more convenient by pushing buttons on the phone rather than by visiting a retail mall hundreds of kilometers away. This is particularly so in China, where e-commerce and especially, m-commerce are essential for reaching consumers in Tier 3 and Tier 4 cities. These consumers spend proportionately more online than consumers living in Tier 1 and Tier 2 cities. Why then should businesses invest in expensive brick-and-mortar stores rather than roll out their products online? All of these factors point to an exploding online market over the next decade.

Back to Alibaba. What are Alibaba's various platforms? How is the company making money?

Alibaba's business model

The company began in 1999 with the web domain Alibaba.com, a business-to-business (B2B) trading platform mostly for small businesses to connect Chinese manufacturers with overseas buyers. Within a few years it became the largest B2B platform of its kind, bringing together importers and exporters from more than 240 countries in the world. Alibaba's B2B trade web site for the China marketplace is www.1688.com. Alibaba also runs AliExpress where small quantities of goods can be bought at wholesale prices. The three marketplaces together have more than 80 million registered users.

Its consumer-to-consumer (C2C) portal Taobao features nearly a billion products and is one of the 20 most-visited websites globally. Alibaba Group's sites account for over 60 per cent of the parcels delivered in China. Alibaba also runs a business-to-consumer (B2C) platform, a shopping search engine. Its affiliate Alipay, a third-party online payment platform, has more than 700 million registered accounts, surpassing PayPal by a wide margin. Alibaba has also invested in cloud computing. Aliyun, Alibaba's cloud computing service, builds platforms for e-commerce data mining, e-commerce data processing, and data customization. Alibaba also owns Yahoo China.

While Alibaba offers all its basic services for free to buyers and sellers, it earns money through online advertisements and extra services it offers clients, such as web site design. Nothing particularly exciting there: many internet companies do the same. However, there is a twist that makes the company dominate its market. It has to do, in part, with the company's brand and reputation, and, in part, with Chinese consumer behavior.

Western shoppers use search engines, such as Google, to find merchandise. For example, they use Google to track the retailer and then follow a link to the retailer's web site or to Amazon. As a result, advertising on Google or using Google's services for pushing the search item high on the display list is highly valuable for companies. Not so in China. First, Alibaba, and specifically its consumer site Taobao, can block the "spiders" that the Chinese search engine Baidu may send out to find the site. It can afford to do this because shoppers know its brand as they are pretty much the only game in town. Moreover, for online and mobile shopping, Chinese consumers may use Alibaba's own shopping search engine. As a result, ads on Alibaba sites are extremely valuable for sellers, and the company can charge a premium for ads. Alibaba thus gets a major part of the revenue that in the West goes to the search engines.

The key is the Chinese consumer

Alibaba, and other companies, are also part of China's shift from an investment-heavy, export-driven model of growth toward a new model focused on consumption and the Chinese consumer. With Chinese consumers, Alibaba seems to be sitting on a gold mine. Alibaba entered the market at the right moment at the right place by providing Chinese consumers today and in the future with the products they desire conveniently and at a good price.

Another Alibaba gold mine in the future may be its detailed knowledge of the middle-class consumer based on access to massive data on their spending habits.

Where to? Soon on Alibaba?

Alibaba has not fully mined these data yet but it may do so in the future.

Starting out as a B2B business, helping small businesses from abroad and within China to access buyers and suppliers, the company is now well positioned for growth and development in China's consumer business.

Being aware of the huge potential of the consumer market, Alibaba has been increasing its mobile shopping and payment platforms. In 2012, the company's C2C marketplace Taobao hosted about 67 per cent of the country's m-commerce transactions. By 2015, Alibaba projects that m-commerce in China will become an industry worth more than USD 41 billion.

But Alibaba is no longer alone: China's mobile carriers are moving into the business as well. In 2013, China Unicom, the second-largest service provider after China Mobile, made a substantial move by hooking up with Korea's SK Group to develop applications for mobile credit card transactions, discount coupons, and prepaid phone services.

The future of companies such as Alibaba is thus not without its risks. The most obvious concern is that the company may grow too fast beyond its core competencies. For example, cloud computing services in China are predicted to grow twelvefold over the next ten years. But there is also significant competition. Not only does Alibaba want to be a major player, but there are other companies such as Tencent, Baidu, and Huawei, all jumping onto the bandwagon. Tencent's Weiyun is being positioned as the third component to its mobile platform that already includes the WeiBo micro-blogging service and the WeiXin (WeChat) group chat service. Baidu has committed USD 1.6 billion in a new data center. Huawei, one of the world's largest telecommunications equipment makers, is launching its global cloud service. Once cloud computing becomes the new arena of competition, for Alibaba the sky may have its limits.

A cultural revolution

The developments in e-commerce, m-commerce, and cloud computing are not only exciting for consumers. They also trigger a cultural revolution within companies in Asia, for example, by ushering in a younger generation of international and edgy leaders. Hiroshi Mikitani, the internet entrepreneur and founder of Rakuten, Japan's largest online retailer, is one of those new leaders—a rebel and game changer against the old management establishment in Japan, or what used to be called "Japan Inc." Mr. Mikitani is trying to get his employees and corporate Japan to speak English. This "Englishization push," as he calls it, is his attempt to build an international corporate culture and to get Rakuten and other Japanese businesses to act like global corporations.

When I met with Mr. Mikitani in Tokyo as part of a conference organized by Columbia Business School's Center on Japanese Economy and Business, his assistant kept calling him "Hiroshi," and he told me that many in his company call him by his nickname, "Miki." During the one-on-one interview on stage, conducted in English, I asked him about how his Englishization push was coming along. He confessed that "it is tough … but I am not giving up … Of course, sometimes it is more productive and efficient to speak in Japanese but I think the upside of communicating in English is much larger than sticking to Japanese … It has totally changed the culture."

A simple change in language can have dramatic consequences because language is a lens through which we perceive the world. In English, it is a *pleasure* to meet somebody; in Japanese, Korean, and Chinese, it is an *honor*. Some languages like Thai use strict gender coding in their grammar. Overall, the English language seems more casual than many languages spoken in Asia. For example, when we conduct business in English, we use the first name (in my case "Bernd") to address somebody; in Asian languages, people address each other by family name (in my case "Schmitt") or full name, often accompanied by a honorific (Chairman, President or, in my case, Professor Schmitt). In Singapore, where I have been living when I wrote this book, the standard is an odd combination: "Professor Bernd." The only way to get this corrected is to say, "Excuse me. My first name is Schmitt." So, now Singaporeans call me "Professor Schmitt." I wonder how I could get them to drop the "professor" and call me by my brand name: SCHMITT.

Of course, just as the Asian consumer may replace the Western consumer as the reference point for business and marketing in the 21st century, maybe, by 2050, the Chinese language rather than English—or perhaps Singlish?—may be the new language of business and commerce.

BIBLIOGRAPHY

SECTION 1

Chapter 1

Janamitra Devan, Micah Rowland, and Jonathan Woetzel, "A Consumer Paradigm for China," *McKinsey Quarterly,* August, 2009.

Tom Doctoroff, *What Chinese Want* (Basingstoke: Palgrave McMillian, 2012).

John Malcolm Dowling, *Future Perspectives on the Economic Development of Asia* (London: World Scientific Publishing, 2008).

N. Nagarash, *Aspects of India's Economic Growth and Reforms* (New Delhi: Academic Foundation, 2006).

Shaun Rein, *The End of Cheap China* (Hoboken: John Wiley and Sons, 2012).

V. Romeschchandra, "Size Counts: China and India Flex Their Consumer Muscle," *Asian Conversations,* 2011.

Shang-Jin Wei, "Will China Slow Down? Not So Fast," *Columbia Ideas at Work: Columbia Business School Blog,* February 28, 2013.

Chapter 2

The story at the beginning of Chapter 2 is fictional; it has been compiled based on similar stories found on the internet.

Michael Andrew and Peng Yali, "The Rise of the Middle Class in Asian Emerging Markets," *KPMG,* April 2012.

A. Banerjee and E. Duflo, "What Is Middle Class About the Middle Classes Around the World?" *Journal of Economic Perspectives,* Vol.22, No.2 (2008): 3–28.

Hannah Beech, "The Scramble for Burma," *Time Magazine,* June 3, 2013.

Natalie Chun, "Middle Class Size in the Past, Present and Future: A Description of Trends in Asia," *Asian Development Bank: Economics Working Paper Series,* No. 217 (2010).

Steffen Dyck, Syetam Hansakul, and Rachna Saxena, "Emerging Asia's Middle Class," *Deutsche Bank Research,* August 21, 2009.

Homi Kharas, "The Emerging Middle Class in Developing Countries," *OECD Development Center: Working Paper, The Brookings Institution.* No. 285 (2010).

Linda Yueh, "Burma: Asia's Last Frontier Is Opening Up," *BBC News Business,* http://bbc.co.uk/news/business-22721804, June 2, 2013.

Chapter 3

Jennifer Aaker and Bernd Schmitt, "Culture-dependent Assimilation and Differentiation of the Self: Preferences for Consumption Symbols in the United States and China," *Journal of Cross-Cultural Psychology,* Vol. 38 (2001): 561–576.

Yuval Atsmon, Jean-Frederic Kuentz, and Jeongmin Seong, "Building Brands in Emerging Markets," *McKinsey Quarterly,* September 2012.

Chi-yue Chiu and Ying yi Hong, *Social Psychology of Culture.* (New York: Psychology Press Kanagawa, Cross, & Markus, 2001).

Adam B. Cohen, "Many Forms of Culture," *American Psychologist,* Vol. 64, No. 3 (2009): 194–204.

William B. Gudykunst, Yuko Matsumoto, Stella Ting-Toomey, Tsukasa Nishida, Kwangsu Kim, and Sam Heyman, "The Influence of Cultural Individualism-Collectivism, Self-construals, and Individual Values on Communication Styles Across Cultures," *Human Communication Research,* Vol. 22 (1996): 510–543.

Geert Hofstede, *Cultures and Organizations: Software of the Mind* (London: McGraw-Hill, 1991).

Geert Hofstede, *Culture's Consequences* (Beverly Hills: SAGE Publications, 1980).

Min-Sun Kim, William F. Sharkey, and Theodore M. Singelis, "The Relationship Between Individuals' Self-construals and Perceived Importance of Interactive Constraints," *International Journal of Intercultural Relations,* Vol. 18 (1994): 117–140.

Kwok Leung and Michael H. Bond, "The Impact of Cultural Collectivism on Reward Allocation," *Journal of Personality and Social Psychology,* Vol. 47 (1984): 793–804.

Hazel R. Markus and Shinobu Kitayama, "Culture and the Self: Implications for Cognition, Emotion, and Motivation," *Psychological Review,* Vol. 20 (1991): 568–579.

Daphna Oyserman, Heather M. Coon, and Markus Kemmelmeier, "Rethinking Individualism and Collectivism: Evaluation of Theoretical Assumptions and Meta-analyses," *Psychological Bulletin,* Vol. 128, No. 1 (2002): 3–72.

Theodore M. Singelis, "The Measurement of Independent and Interdependent Self-construals," *Personality and Social Psychology Bulletin,* Vol. 20 (1994): 580–591.

Nancy Y. Wong and Aaron C. Ahuvia, "Personal Taste and Family Face: Luxury Consumption in Confucian and Western Societies," *Psychology and Marketing,* Vol. 15 No. 5 (1998): 423–441.

Chapter 4

ACI, *Pan-Asian WAVE Consumer Study*. (Principal investigator: Professor Rajeev Batra, University of Michigan), 2013.

Arthur Asa Berger, "Postmodernism." In Marcel Danesi (Ed.), *Encyclopedia of Media and Communications*. Toronto: University of Toronto Press, 2013 (pp. 525-530)

Shoma Munshi (Ed.), *Images of the 'Modern Women' in Asia: Global Media, Local Meanings* (Richmond: Routledge Publishing, 2001).

Andrew Nathan, "Patterns of Traditionalism in East Asia," Paper presented at How East Asian View Democracy Conference, Taipei, December 8–9, 2003.

Piyush Sharma, Cindy M. Y. Chung, M. Krishna Erramilli, and Bharadhwaj Sivakumaran, "Challenges of Marketing to Asian Consumers: Exploring the Influence of Different Cultures, Lifestyles, and Values on Consumer Behavior in Asia," In Henry Wai-chung Yeung (Ed.), *Handbook of Research on Asian Business* (Cheltenham: Edward Elgar Publishing Limited, 2007).

Robert J. Shepherd, "Consumer Culture in East Asia," In Dale Southerton (Ed.), *Encyclopedia of Consumer Culture* (Thousand Oaks: SAGE Publications, 2011).

Unknown, "Mass Affluent Consumers in Southeast Asia," *Roland Berger Strategy Consultants,* June 11, 2013.

Unknown, "Nielsen Finds Asian Shopaholics," *Daily Research News Online,* http://www.mrweb.com/drno/news5730.htm, July 19, 2006.

Unknown, "Shopaholics Wanted," *The Economist,* June 25, 2009.

Chapter 5

ACI, *Pan-Asian WAVE Consumer Study*. (Principal investigator: Professor Rajeev Batra, University of Michigan), 2013.

Julien Cayla and Eric Arnould, "Ethnographic Stories for Market Learning," Journal of Marketing, Vol 77, (2013) 1-16.

Paul Magnone, "4 Big Data Trends That Change Everything," *Forbes,* June 22, 2013.

Naresh K. Malhotra, *Marketing Research: An Applied Orientation (6th Edition)* (Upper Saddle River: Prentice-Hall, 2009).

Carmen Nobel, "What Neuroscience Tells Us About Consumer Desire," Harvard Business School Blog, March 26, 2012.

SECTION 2

Chapter 6

Andrew Delios and Kulwant Singh, *Strategies for Success in Asia* (Singapore: John Wiley and Sons, 2005).

Wayne S. DeSarbo, C. Anthony di Benedetto, Michael Song, and Indrajit Sinha, "Revisiting the Miles and Snow Strategic Framework: Uncovering Interrelationships Between Strategic Types, Capabilities, Environmental Uncertainty, and Firm Performance," *Strategic Management Journal,* Vol. 26 (2005): 47–74.

Huw McKay and Ligang Song, "China As a Global Manufacturing Powerhouse: Strategic Considerations and Structural Adjustment," *China and World Economy,* Vol. 18, No. 1 (2010): 1–32.

Raymond E. Miles and Charles Curtis Snow, *Organizational Strategy, Structure, and Process* (New York: McGraw-Hill, 1978).

Chapter 7

Yuval Atsmon and Max Magni, "Meet the Chinese Consumer of 2020," *McKinsey Quarterly,* March, 2012.

David Court and Laxman Narasimhan, "Capturing the World's Emerging Middle Class," *McKinsey Quarterly,* July, 2010.

C. K. Prahalad, *The Fortune at the Bottom of the Pyramid* (Upper Saddle River: Prentice-Hall, 2010).

Eric Simanis, "At the Base of the Pyramid," *The Wall Street Journal,* June 15, 2012.

Unknown, "What is the Right Entry Point for Emerging Markets: Targeting Customers at the Bottom or the Middle of the Pyramid," *Harvard Business Review Singapore Sessions,* 2012.

Chapter 8

Todd Guild, "Think Regionally, Act Locally: Four Steps to Reaching the Asian Consumer," *McKinsey Quarterly,* September 2009.

Raoul Oberman, Richard Dobbs, Arief Budiman, Fraser Thompson, and Morten Rossé, "The Archipelago Economy: Unleashing Indonesia's Potential," *McKinsey and Company,* September 2012.

Bernd Schmitt, "Who Is the Chinese Consumer? Segmentation in the People's Republic of China," *European Management Journal,* Vol. 15, No. 2 (1997): 191–194.

Chapter 9

Julian Cayla and Giana Eckardt, "Asian Brands and the Shaping of a Transnational Imagined Community," *Journal of Consumer Research,* Vol. 35 (2008).

Radha Chadha and Paul Husband, *The Cult of the Luxury Brand: Inside Asia's Love Affair with Luxury* (London, UK: Nicholas Brealey International, 2006).

Martin Roll, *Asian Brand Strategy: How Asia Builds Strong Brands* (Basingstoke: Palgrave McMillian, 2006).

Bernd Schmitt and Yigang Pan, "Managing Brand Identities in the Asia-Pacific Region," *California Management Review,* Vol. 36, No. 4 (1994).

Bernd Schmitt, *Customer Experience Management* (Hoboken: John Wiley and Sons, 2003).

Bernd Schmitt, *Experiential Marketing* (New York: The Free Press, 1999).

Paul Temporal, *Branding in Asia* (Hoboken: John Wiley and Sons, 2000).

L. Zarantonello, K. Jedidi, and B. H. Schmitt, "Functional and Experiential Routes to Persuasion: An Analysis of Advertising in Emerging vs. Developed Markets,"

International Journal of Research in Marketing: Special Issue on Marketing in Emerging Markets, Vol. 30, No 1 (2013): 46–56.

SECTION 3

Christopher Lovelock and Jochen Wirtz, *Services Marketing: People, Technology, Strategy (7th Edition)* (Boston: Prentice-Hall, 2008).

Chapter 15

Juro Osawa, "Huawei Set to Launch New Smartphone," *The Wall Street Journal,* June 17, 2013.

Bill Powell, "Can Apple Win over China?" *CNN Money,* October 29, 2012.

Bernd Schmitt, "Samsung's Next Frontier," *Columbia CaseWorks.*

Stan Shih, *Smile and Beat Your Own Path: Stan Shih's Smiling Philosophy* (in print).

Unknown, "From Guard Shack to Global Giant," *The Economist,* January 12, 2013.

Unknown, "The Mighty, Fallen," *The Economist,* March 3, 2011.

Unknown, "Now for the Soft Part," *The Economist,* October 6, 2012.

Sterling Wong, "Riding the Korean Wave: How K-Pop Stars Have Helped Samsung to the Top in Asia," *Yahoo! Singapore Finance,* February 1, 2013.

Chapter 16

David Brooks, "The Romantic Advantage," *The New York Times,* May 30, 2013.

Natasha Khan and Frederik Balfour, "Richemont's Shanghai Tang to Double Chinese Stores As Luxury Demand Climbs," *Bloomberg,* October 6, 2011.

Jing Qiu and Ruiming Lin, "New Trends Among Young Chinese Consumers," *SERI Quarterly,* January 2013.

Chapter 17

Jimmy Hsiung, "The Rise of the Brothers Wei and the Ting Hsin International Group," *China Post,* February 6, 2012.

Alison Tudor, Laurie Burkitt, and Mike Esterl, "PepsiCo to Sell China Bottling Operations," *The Wall Street Journal,* November 4, 2011.

Unknown, "Ting Hsin Is Largest Taipei 101 Shareholder," *China Post,* July 19, 2009.

Chapter 18

Anshuman Daga, "Sky's the Limit? Southeast Asia Budget Airlines Bet Big on Growth," *Reuters,* March 23, 2013.

Thomas Lawton, "How Legacy Airlines Can Be Competitive Again," *US News and World Report,* March 23, 2012.

Unknown, "Cheap and Cheerful," *The Economist,* May 22, 2003.

Adelene Wong, "Asia's Budget Airlines: Only Fittest Will Survive," *TodayOnline,* June 10, 2013.

Chapter 19

Russell Arthur Smith and Judy Siguaw, *Strategic Hospitality Management: An Asian Initiative* (Singapore: John Wiley and Sons, 2010).

Nancy Trejos, "U.S. Hotels Expand Their Reach into Asia," *USA Today,* November 16, 2011.

Unknown, "W Hotels Worldwide Announces Asia Expansion Plans," *Hotelmanagement.net,* www.hotelmanagement.net, April 23, 2013.

Chapter 20

Mike Adams, "Asian Beauty Industry on Growth Trend," *Natural News,* April 2, 2005.

Ruth Holliday, Gender, Globalization, and Cosmetic Surgery in South Korea. *Body and Society*, Vol. 18, No. 2 (2012): 58-81.

Megan Puhl, "Puhl's Provocative Perceptions on People, Place, and Planning," Megan Puhl's Blog, August 3, 2012.

Andrew Salmon, "South Korea's Cosmetic Surgery Craze Creates Identikit Beauty Queens," *South China Morning Post,* May 14, 2013.

Ahn Sol, "Asians Drive the Premium Skin Care Market," *Emerging Markets Insight,* 9–15.

Unknown, "The Dynamic Korean Wave," **www.In-Cosmeticsasia.com.**

Unknown, "Plastic Surgery Stats and Medical Tourists," *Seoul Touch Up,* http://www.seoultouchup.com/korean-plastic-surgery-statistics-medical-tourists.

Chapter 21

Bruce Einhorn, "Alibaba's Jack Ma Is Moving on with an IPO Looming," *Bloomberg Businessweek*, January 15, 2013.

Unknown, "The Alibaba Phenomenon," *The Economist,* **March 23, 2013.**

Unknown, "Surfing South-East Asia's Powerful Digital Wave," *Accenture Report,* 2012.

Unknown, "The World's Greatest Bazaar," *The Economist,* March 23, 2013.

ABOUT THE AUTHOR

Bernd Schmitt has more than 20 years of experience in Asia. As professor, he held appointments in China, Hong Kong, Singapore, and South Korea. As researcher, he studied and published articles on consumer segmentation, corporate identity, brand naming, and communications in emerging markets. As speaker and consultant, he has worked with more than 50 highly esteemed companies worldwide, including Asian companies and multinational corporations in the region such as Samsung, Sony, Shanghai Jahwa, Lotte, Sunstar, China Eastern Airlines, Amore Pacific, and Unilever (among others).

From 2011 until 2013, while writing this book, Schmitt was a visiting professor at Nanyang Technological University in Singapore. During this two-year period, as Executive Director of ACI (the Institute on Asian Consumer Insight), he set up all key programs and initiatives of the institute. At Columbia Business School in New York, he is the Robert D. Calkins Professor of International Business and Faculty Director of the Center on Global Brand Leadership.

Schmitt has authored, co-authored, and edited more than 100 academic articles, books, and case studies. His business books—including *Experiential Marketing, Customer Experience Management, Big Think Strategy,* and *Happy Customers Everywhere*—have been translated into more than 20 languages, and have helped businesses successfully connect with their customers in meaningful ways.

He is a frequent keynote speaker at renowned conferences worldwide. In Asia he has spoken to audiences in Japan, South Korea, China, Hong Kong, Macau, Singapore, Malaysia, Indonesia, the Philippines, and India. He has appeared on BBC, CNBC, CNBC-Asia, Channel NewsAsia, CNN, and NHK.